ADAM HUTCHISON

RISK V
REWARD

THE EMPLOYEE-EMPLOYER CONUNDRUM

ADAM HUTCHISON

RISK V
REWARD

THE EMPLOYEE-EMPLOYER CONUNDRUM

MEREO
Cirencester

Mereo Books

1A The Wool Market Dyer Street Cirencester Gloucestershire GL7 2PR
An imprint of Memoirs Publishing www.mereobooks.com

Risk vs. Reward: 978-1-86151-608-4

First published in Great Britain in 2016
by Mereo Books, an imprint of Memoirs Publishing

The address for Memoirs Publishing Group Limited can be found at
www.memoirspublishing.com

The Memoirs Publishing Group Ltd Reg. No. 7834348

The Memoirs Publishing Group supports both The Forest Stewardship Council®
(FSC®) and the PEFC® leading international forest-certification organisations. Our
books carrying both the FSC label and the PEFC® and are printed on FSC®-certified
paper. FSC® is the only forest-certification scheme supported by the leading
environmental organisations including Greenpeace. Our paper procurement policy
can be found at www.memoirspublishing.com/environment

Typeset in 12/18pt Bembo
by Wiltshire Associates Publisher Services Ltd. Printed and bound in Great Britain
by Printondemand-Worldwide, Peterborough PE2 6XD

CONTENTS

Acknowledgements
About the author
Introduction

ACKNOWLEDGEMENTS

I would like to thank people who have helped me put this book together, not only by giving their support in writing it up but by giving me the general push to write it in the first place. Many of us have ideas - the biggest issue is usually the confidence and the drive to execute them. It had always been a long-standing ambition of mine to put my experiences into words, so I thank Danielle, my wife, my inspiration and 'The General', for ordering me to get on and complete it. I would also like to thank all those I have worked for and alongside, or employed or trained, as those experiences, whether good or bad, have enabled me to develop in my career.

About the author

Adam Hutchison has spent the last two decades working in both the private and public sectors, operating within corporate and SME environments, working at the operational level on the front line and doing everything from running departments to operating his own businesses. During this time his experiences have always raised the same key question: 'What makes a business great?' The answer every time is 'people'. Although this is a huge subject, the word 'people' or 'person' is paramount to a business. This book explores the dos and don'ts of people - why do we employ? How do we employ? What cultures are right? How are cultures created? The involvement of people is in direct correlation to the development of a business; whether it's five people or 5000, the message needs to be the same.

If we all woke up on a Monday morning and wanted to go to work, what a difference it would make. How do we get to this stage in our careers? It's different for everyone, but fun, passion, desire and respect are key drivers to the achievement of synergy within a business. Hopefully some of the experiences and research described in this book can help you and your business to form a path to great success through people.

The real point is that human beings need rewards to function, not only in life but in work. Positive comments drive attitudes and behaviours. Forget these simple rules at your own risk!

Introduction

Dun dun dun dun dun dun dun goes the sound of my generic fruit based devices' alarm at 6.15 am. There it goes again like a monotonous merry-go-round, taunting me with its repetitiveness. Monday morning again. But does it really matter which day it is? The days are always the same - that feeling of déjà vu or inevitability if you will.

'Do I want to get up and see the Viking?' I ask myself. This is the nickname I give to my long-standing leviathan of a managing director. As ever, I begin wondering what niceties I will be served as I enter the office today, early of course, as I do every day, but especially on a Monday, as this is the day for the weekly sales briefing and a general rollicking session, regardless of performance.

It wasn't only I who felt this way, which was a concern, seeing as that as a sales director my role was essentially to lead the briefing with the aim of motivating my team for the week ahead. This feeling of impending dread seemed almost mutual across the 50 or so members of my team. I was supposed to be the leader of this group, motivated to drive them into a new week. However, many people would be late or call in sick or have a childcare problem, any excuse to miss the early Monday morning humiliation. It seemed that punishment for lateness was preferred to a public slander for poor performance – lesser of two evils, I suppose.

It seemed I entered each week with trepidation, and even I, as part of the senior management team, felt concern. Would it be a 'good morning'? Would it be a 'how was your weekend?' I very much doubted it. I would no doubt be met with a barrage of remarks regarding last week's performance and my expected level of achievement for this week. So as I was saying – should I get up, or should I just roll over and stay right here in my nice warm bed?

Why did I decide to write this book? Because that was how I often used to feel when I was working as a sales director for a large telecommunications organisation. That was my moment of clarity, my epiphany. I decided that work had become my life. It was then that I told myself I would no longer go to work feeling like that. Why should I? I now ask myself the same thing every Sunday night before I rest my head for another week - do I want to get up tomorrow? And if the answer is no, then I change something, or I do something else to ensure I will not feel the same way the following week.

Now wherever you sit as an individual, whether you're a business owner, director, manager or employee, you'll know that we have all felt like this. What I hope to achieve with this book is to help you realise that at some point everyone has felt like this, so do we really want ourselves, and more importantly our workforce, to be feeling the same way? If they do, will we get the best out of them? Of course we won't. As we all know, our employees are our most important assets, regardless of the size or style of business. No organisation rises or falls without the influence of the employees on which they rely so much.

So why is it that time and time again in my career as an employee, business owner and consultant I have found that most businesses continually fail to focus on the operational level of the business? The roots are the most important part of a tree, yet it is so often seen as a risk to maintain your business in this way rather than opting for quick-fix solutions based on sayings like 'square pegs in round holes' or 'the grass is always greener' (an over-used phrase in all walks of life). What always baffled me was that the solution was so obvious; you can spend less money and create more if you focus begins within your business. So why do so many choose not to? The truth is - because it seems like too much hard work. Yet hard work has always brought results. Hard work focusing on the processes, which underpin your business, will pay off in the long run – short-term pain is truly long-term gain. Even if the long-term goal is to sell the business, these values will carry it through all forms of change.

My career has progressed from corporate and government operations in multinational telecoms to SMEs in both the private and the public sectors. Year on year I have encountered the same issues and the same problems for managers and business owners alike. They failed to truly focus on the single most important factor in any business - its employer-employee relationship. Regardless of position or process, the employees within an organisation will always make or break its success. It's down to culture, motivation and loyalty. Relationships are the key foundation of how we carry ourselves as human beings - our relationships with partners, family and friends - so it's no real shock that the same fundamentals can be true in the work environment.

Hasn't it all been said before? Over the years I have read a plethora of papers, books and articles on the subjects of leadership, motivation and management. My aim was to encapsulate this, linked with enthusiasm for the importance of the subject matter. I hope this is what I have achieved. I'm passionate, as are many, about ensuring that the workplace becomes as important a part of everyone's life as any other aspect. Businesses built on passion have always succeeded; the passion at the top must be allowed to filter through the business. This is much easier within small businesses or those where the founder is still within the organisation, but that doesn't mean it cannot be achieved in other situations. I have attended so many seminars where entrepreneurs talk of their businesses success stories, all driven by their enthusiasm for their idea. If this forms the lifeblood of a business, success will just happen, and work will become a hobby - and what is better than that, seeing as it takes up 75% of our lives?

. In this book I will explore my thoughts and those of others in the field and give simple tips to help business professionals create a driven, loyal workforce, all working towards a common group-generated goal. I wanted to write a book from a professional's perspective taking into account views from professional fields, including human resourcing, but showing how inherently businesses miss this key aspect which can instantly change their fortunes. Some businesses I have worked with have broken new barriers in their development, bringing all-round success and wellbeing to their work environment. This has of course improved profitability growth for the organisation. Why? Simple - because everyone cares!

The real point is that human beings need rewards to function, not only in life but in work. Positive comments drive attitudes and behaviours, so you forget these simple rules at your own risk!

1

THE TRADE OFF – RISK V. REWARD

Let's start by looking in simple terms at what risks and rewards are. Let's look at the different definitions of these words, as this will help focus on the rest of the book. Many businesses see risks day in day out, but sometimes it's the failure to reward in the right way that is the risk and rewarding the right processes can help reduce the risks to the business. So to the dictionary we go:

RISK
Noun:
i. The possibility of incurring misfortune or loss; hazard

Verb:
i. To expose to danger or loss; hazard
ii. To act in spite of the possibility of loss.

Note that risk refers to possibilities, not certainties. This is surely important when thinking of business risk. Perception is everything. To be mindful that it may happen will enable you to plan for any possible risks. In any business planning process, risks will be highlighted and plans will be made to address possible risks if they arise. More often than not the risks identified are generic – in recruitment, for example, the risk will no doubt be analysed in the number of people vs. the roles to be filled. Easy fix there, we have a tick in the box. But do we? The recruitment risk is much bigger than this and can become a laborious task if the plans for recruitment are not specific to the type of culture and people you need in the business in the first place. Therefore this part of business planning needs to be much better thought out and certainly not generically focused on numbers and roles. These issues will be discussed further as we go through the chapters.

REWARD

Noun:

i. *Something given in return for a deed or service rendered*

ii. *A sum of money offered, esp. for help in finding/returning something*

iii. *Profit or return*

iv. *Something received in return for goods*

v. *Any pleasant event that follows a response and therefore increases the likelihood of the response recurring in the future*

Verb:

i. *(Transitive) to give (something) to (someone), esp. in gratitude for a service rendered; recompense*

The definition above refers to inherent themes that can be identified, themes which relate to all businesses. Awareness of this, and then using this awareness to implement change within your business, will in the long term increase productivity and efficiency, which itself increases the long term business goal - profitability and growth.

Exercise

Take this opportunity right now as an exercise to list the risks to your business. As we work through the book, implementing techniques will enable these risks to be mapped into potential rewards, ensuring a more efficient, better-motivated workforce and utilising less management time. So put the book to one side, take a blank piece of paper and highlight some of the risks you feel you face in general as a business. Many of these may involve your staff, departmental issues, client issues or financial restraints. All are important and all are relevant. This is not a SWOT analysis, nor is it a demotivating list of the weaknesses of your organisation - it is an opportunity for you to realise the risks that may be in front of you right now.

An exhaustive list may make you feel you are being harsh on yourself, while no list at all seems a little blinkered. You should list at least five items relating to areas within the range of your business. Once you have them, remember them. They will be covered in the following chapters, helping you to create imaginative ideas to work through these challenges and breathe new life into your businesses development. Business performance is a function of your organisation's health, and a pool of loyal, talented employees is paramount. The focus on employee performance is a function of the competence and commitment shown by the business in response to this. Businesses cannot expect their employees to drive this initiative - if they could, surely they could run their own companies without the need to work within one.

If you are an MD/CEO or leader/manager, what are you doing to enhance employee performance and improve the health of the company? A risk you may have identified in the brief exercise above may be the lack of loyal talented employees. Another may be how their performance is formally measured, for example.

Performance measurement is so often associated with sales functions within a business, but levels of performance are vital in all areas of a business, so finding ways to measure each department will help create a more fluid plan for success. Each department can have a reward scheme in place for measuring how they are performing against the measures you have put in place. As we go through the book, as highlighted by the definitions above, these rewards do not have to be monetary and on some occasions the rewards will cost nothing yet will achieve great boosts to your workforce. Having plans for each department's performance is a key part of developing each part of the business. Why would it just be the sales functions which need a pick-me-up to do the job effectively when other departments also hold the keys to unlocking potential growth?

2

THE TRADE-OFF CONUNDRUM

Whether you are an entrepreneur beginning in business or an experienced managing director, leading employees towards a common goal should always be high on the agenda. I always talk of trade-offs, because the common practice is for people in these positions to believe that there is constant conflict between themselves and their employees. During my mentoring I was told that 'staff are like children'. Not having children, it did intrigue me as to what the statement really meant. I was led to believe that it meant employees need clear guidelines and discipline on a daily basis to succeed. This can be interpreted in different ways, and how it is interpreted differs greatly.

The meaning of 'managing performance' is usually misunderstood by managers, who think it means being in control, or acting as the parent in the room. We have all been there, we have all carried out this approach. Did it work? Ask yourself this, because my answer is clear, no it did not! It will never work. Going back to my introduction, the business in question was run by fear, and fear is a sure way to create unease. How can any workforce operate with the feeling of unease? It is a false economy. I found myself working harder to repair the unease than on focusing on what our measured outcomes should have been and the business performance.

So when I talk of a trade-off, this is it - leadership is about evaluating what we are doing right and what we are doing wrong. Accept that you have to trade with your teams to find the best approach to achieving a common goal. As with children, you can't force them to do anything. This only creates further resistance to the outcome and makes the parents' role or in this case the leader's role, much more difficult in the long run.

Gone are days of the 'whip and stick' mentality brought from aggressive sales agencies in the 1980s. An example I heard one day from a senior executive in a manufacturing firm in the UK was as follows:

Owner: How are the guys today, are they moaning about me?

Manager: Yes sir, they are, following this morning's meeting.

Owner: Good, I must be doing my job then!

Owner walks off in a smug fashion.

This type of response is still commonplace in business, a scary thought, as so many leaders constantly seek to create a sense of distance between themselves and their employees. This is a mistake founded on past experiences in their own employment, built on what I have heard referred to as the 'Alpha Wolf' approach (by Dr Steven

Peters in the book The Chimp Paradox). Let's take the same premise but turn it on to a personal level and place the previous conversation in a personal/social situation.

Just think about that for a second. Would this type of conversation help to get something done? Would you expect people to want to do you a favour or carry out a task for you if the expectation is that this is how you should be? The answer is simple – no, it wouldn't. We would not act in this way, because it is simply rude. So why do we believe we should treat people differently because we are at work? This is a common mistake and the start of where employees and employers begin their long-term conflict. Sadly this only ends up with a lack of productivity followed by a sense of demotivation, driven by a lack of mutual respect for one another at the crucial levels within an organisation.

What we are all looking for as human beings is a sense of connection, a need for belonging and self-gratification for a good honest day's work. Reflect back to the opening paragraph again - do you think I felt motivated to go to work and deliver? No of course not. I did as much as I could to get the job done but no more than that, no extra mile. And did I have respect for my superior to the point where I would follow him through thick and thin? No. This is down to respect for each other in the workplace, the starting point for any relationship building.

Nearly every employee works for monetary reward but employees want to work for more than a pay cheque: they want to work with, and for, people they respect and admire, and who respect and admire them in return. Hence the need for a kind word, a quick discussion about family, an informal conversation to ask if an employee needs any help. These moments are much more important than group meetings or formal evaluations. A true sense of connection is personal.

That's why exceptional leaders show that they see and appreciate the person, not just the worker, and see value in the connection between them.

The theme of respect is always open to interpretation, but in the workplace it can be offered in simple ways, sometimes just by listening to people's opinions. This does not mean they have to be adopted; just the opportunity to openly share views on an organisation is a great form of respect. *'When people talk, listen completely. Most people never listen.'* - Ernest Hemingway. This is inherently true of most people. Listening to your employees shows you value their opinions, which in turn creates a more cohesive working environment.

Listening is the foundation of any good relationship. Great leaders listen to what their customers and prospects want and need, and to the challenges those customers face. They listen to colleagues and are open to new ideas. They listen to shareholders, investors and competitors. So why not add your own trusted employees to this group? After all they will be taking on the lion's share of the work. Those who are successful rely on the wealth of employees to make their visions a reality.

3

AGGRESSION = NEGATIVITY

Who has seen *Glengarry Glen Ross* and *Boiler Room*, two of my favourite 'how not to do it' sales movies? I have used them in seminars and training sessions over and over, but not for the reasons you would expect.

This brings us to some observations I have made in my time, and, sad to say, of mistakes I have made myself. I have fallen into erroneous ways and failed on more than one occasion to get things right in the eyes of my team members. Some areas to consider are as follows. You will have your own ideas, but give these two simple approaches a thought.

A simple 'Hello'

As touched on in the previous section, perception of how managers deal with their teams is paramount, so ensure there is less aggression in the delivery. I personally experienced as an employed manager what it was like to be on the receiving end of derogatory comments from your seniors. All this achieved was to drive demotivated behaviour. Having experienced this feeling of not wanting to deliver for someone, it became easy for me when running my own businesses to discuss with others how negative this can be.

Sadly, if you have not been through this, you can become blinkered to the fact that as an owner you are doing it wrong. The phrase 'delusions of grandeur' is often used, which I associate with aggression. Owner/directors who have either developed a business themselves or worked in a very limited environment may not have the experience of dealing with many employees or even with many colleagues - this is lost in the drive to fulfil their initial vision. As the business grows and more employees come on board, a sense of over-importance begins to develop. The poor treatment of your employees becomes so evident that demotivation can creep in. Owners do need to be in strong control, but not to the detriment of their own end goals.

Simple ways of maintaining good staff relations include:

- Saying hello in the morning.
- Asking how someone is, about their family or how they spent their weekend.
- Learning the key points about their personal lives.

Simple interaction can go a long way to creating sustainable value with your employees.

During my time working in the UK private healthcare sector, which is largely seen as a high-turnover, low-expectation industry, I constantly tried to find ways to engage with my staff group through initiatives such as

Employee of the Month, Employee of the Year, performance incentives etc. These all failed to be met with any real enthusiasm, and I couldn't understand why. It had worked in corporate environments, marketing teams and call centres - what was I doing wrong?

I spoke with long-standing managers within the business and asked them for their thoughts on this possible engagement. What came back was interesting. They asked me to attend staff meetings from time to time, thank my staff for their hard work and organise more regular team gatherings. This seemed all too simple - why was I thinking so big? The reason was expectation. During the feedback sessions I found that people within the business enjoyed chatting with me as the owner; they welcomed a simple 'hello' or 'how's your day going?' This is evident in all industries. Sometimes just talking with your staff will be all the engagement they need. Never forget the personal touch - be visible, be approachable.

So over the following months I took a regular quarterly spot in staff meetings and made the effort to engage with staff on each site visit throughout the year. I began to see a change in attitude towards the senior management. The workforce began to feel part of the structure. This was not to blur lines of management - the workforce still understood the hierarchy - but the fact that there was more engagement even on these simple terms, created instant gratification for their contribution, which then reflected in the quality of their work following on. Remember, being more approachable galvanises your workforce.

Giving direction

Direction is next on the agenda of simple pointers towards

breeding a positive environment and removing the aggression. If you want someone to do something, it's best to understand what your outcomes are, and what they will be for the employees doing the task. Make people become part of the process - don't demand of people without justification. If the goal is shared then success is more likely. The passion you have as an owner for a project/product/customer/situation should be ingrained into those around you.

It's a mistake to bark orders around and expect results; this in many situations brings an initial spike in performance, but the long-term risk is demotivation, which results in loss of employee engagement, which results ultimately in having to re-recruit. This is of course win-win for the recruitment consultant, but fail-fail for you and your business. Recruitment should always be seen as a last resort.

We will look at recruitment later, but the mindset around it should be changed so that you recruit only when you have no alternative, or are actively growing, creating a need for more people in desired areas to achieve the goals set out. You should set a precedent - each time you need to go a recruitment consultant or agency, ask yourself, 'Why am I recruiting?' The answer is very important. Is it to replace someone who has left because if so, there is a problem somewhere? This needs addressing each time. Why did the person leave? Ask yourself what you can improve to ensure that people stay with the business. Ask - did we do everything we could to ensure that person could grow and be successful with us rather than go elsewhere?

More often than not this is linked to personal management and delivery of requests made. Aggression is often seen as necessary when it comes to managing people, but why? Ask why you are being aggressive. Is it related to something within my control rather than theirs?

Employees are duty bound to follow by example when delivering on instructions. If you as an owner are not clearly following the processes you have laid down - or worse, have no processes in place - then your expectation levels need to be lower. The aggression is just frustrations aired. Aggression is just loss of control, and loss of control means loss of respect.

People can only deliver against clear objectives laid down in the first place by their leaders. This helps with the measurement of tasks long term. But being aggressive in delivery will reduce any chance of a sound, measured outcome from any task.

Creating clear objectives for yourself and those around you will help achieve this, though well-thought-out processes to clear outcomes, creating the route map to a goal, are key to achieving it. As with sports teams, tactics employed are there to deliver the achievement, or end result if you like. In business it's the same; your employees need clear directions and tactics to compete in their environment.

Whip and stick

In Chapter 1 we briefly mentioned the premise. This is a notion that has developed more often in sales teams where leaders believed that using the stick to drive a workforce was the only way. In the 1990s, when sales teams were usually led by strong, autocratic leaders, the belief was, the more stick the better. People were driven to achieve by the fear of what the consequence would be. Does that sound familiar?

This approach is notoriously a characteristic of what's

known as the 'Alpha Wolf' (referred to by Prof. Stephen Peters in his book *The Chimp Paradox,* 2012), which refers in terms of employment to someone who believes in his or her own ability to drive up performance through fear. As awareness of employee rights and wellbeing intensifies, it is easy to see that these tactics simply don't work any more - no one likes a bully, and we learn this at a very young age. So what makes us think these initiatives have a place in the work environment? We are brought up believing bullying is bad, yet in practice it goes on right through life. Approaches need to change - if this is you, then focusing on what to do next is the key to success in working with your employees.

A concept I have used when training sales teams was the 'black line of doom - green line of joy'. This is the idea that more often than not, the process of managing employees is very simple, as employees have only two mindsets - the avoidance of pain and the achievement of success. The pain can come in many formats, but ultimately it is the consequence set out by the management structure of failure or non-compliance. The other end of this is the achievement of success or joy, which is again simple – it's the employee looking to achieve, which is usually determined by understanding his or her personal drivers. Rewards can then be mapped to those drivers. This will be explored further in later chapters when we explore further development planning. Finding a clear definition of where you as a leader and your employees sit on this scale is important. No leader will succeed long term if employees are ruled by fear!

Table 1 illustrates the 'black line of doom - green line of joy' idea:

TABLE 1

BLACK LINE OF DOOM	GREEN LINE OF JOY
Disciplinary/Warnings	**Achievement of targets**
Personal failure	**Commissions/Incentives**
Lower Income	**Promotions**
Name and shame	**Competition**
Public dressing down	**Personal Development**

The table only illustrates examples; it is important for you to sit down during your downtime as leader and write your own table showing what you feel your employees believe sits in which column. It is so important to reflect on what is going on around you from a helicopter viewpoint and to step outside the normal business activity, and it can become some of the best time spent, even if it's just for a short period each month. This is something you should do regularly, to give a clear indicator of how to manage your teams effectively and get the most out of them. It will create clear objectives, and evaluation of your own performance is a must.

This exercise may identify whether the business does offer clear consequences, and conversely, if it offers the most effective incentives for people to give the business 100%.

Displaying clearly how the business is driven, the key is to understand that the modern business it should be led predominantly by the Green Line of Joy and as little as possible by the Black Line of Doom. The black line not only creates more work – it gives you an unmotivated workforce. It sounds simple in theory, though in practice it's so easy to slip into the idea of being autocratic, demanding more of your business by force rather than cohesive direction.

At no point am I saying that any of the items in the black line are wrong as they are formal employment law processes, but any leader/manager who has ever had to experience these journeys know they are notoriously time-consuming, expensive and frustrating. So why do them, if they can be avoided through a change in approach?

This whip and stick approach is clearly one of the least productive ways of working and will never bring enhanced results, only fear. Fear of failure and fear of the leadership mechanism in the business is a great risk, as it focuses a lot of negative energy towards staff, increasing the risk of creating a lack of motivation. If you are adopting this type of management style, you will become tired of the negative nature of the approach, creating further lack of productivity across the organisation.

You won't make things better by attacking others around you. You need to develop constructive behaviours by offering support, in order to breed improvement amongst the people around you. This will reduce the risk for the business when dealing with possible resulting HR issues, which are less likely to resonate in the first place.

What better way to motivate staff than through measured support? As human beings we welcome support in our endeavours, and being offered it in the workplace enhances loyalty to the organisation. Ongoing encouragement acts as a carrot to employees, something we all need to enable us to respond positively to a given situation. Personally I refer to this notion as the 'T' junction

- you reach a point with your employees when using this approach that they will either improve through the support you offered or leave, because they don't want to improve. Either way it's a success. Not everyone fits the model, but the process becomes easily manageable and measurable.

So referring back to our initial exercise on risk, the employee risk should now be clear. How many employees are already at the 'T' junction, and what are your next steps? How many of your teams are getting the support to move forward consistently, and how many of them come to work to focus on the achievements rather than the fear - are they appropriately motivated?

What you have to remember is that you do not want to operate a compliance v. motivation workforce. People may well comply with the stick approach within an autocratic leadership structure, but it will not motivate them.

4

MOTIVATING YOUR WORKFORCE

Motivation is misunderstood by many businesses and it's a huge subject about which people make many assumptions. Yes, money is a good motivator, sometimes the best, but it is short-lived and it is not the only way your employees can be motivated. The key to motivating people is understanding some of the following aspects:

■ Current situation.

■ Desires.

■ Mindset.

Why do we need to understand such things? Because we want to be motivated, but in different ways. Part of any recruitment journey should be to understand in advance what your people need to get the best out of them. If you don't know this, how can you ensure you are ready to drive people the right way? The risk is that you could be motivating them all with the same carte blanche approach and getting very mixed responses.

Each employee needs a workflow which matches the best way to keep them growing within a company. Some are motivated by money, some by promotion, some by wellbeing and some purely by environment - and what many find hard to believe is that some of the things that motivate them could cost you nothing.

You can find out more by mapping each of your people to their key motivators. This can be done in a 1:1 environment, during development plans (discussed later in the book), although ideally this should be done when recruiting. Why? Because you can see whether this fits existing employee profiles, reducing the need for multiple channels of motivation. Worse, you could be implementing expensive new approaches not already undertaken just to get the most out of one new addition. That may not be implemented for whatever reason in the long run anyway.

Sometimes too little is done in the early stages when employing people, which over time creates more cost for the business. A little more groundwork with your people from the offset will reduce staff turnover from lack of motivation.

In positions where I have offered consultancy work to businesses I have come across very simple oversights which have cost businesses dearly because they were not dealt with efficiently. They mainly occur when someone was first employed. Remember, a new employee is scoping you out as an employer just as you are them as a new member of the team. They want to feel valued, they want the right facilities and equipment, the right location - the list goes on. What better way to show them this by than by asking simple questions during the recruitment process such as:

- What motivates you?
- What do you expect from me as an employer if you are successful?
- What does work mean to you and your lifestyle?
- What is your plan for the next five years? Not in work but personal goals.

You can create your own questions, adding more if you like, but this will help you get the idea. Know your people inside out before you take them on as employees. The long-term results will be significant and in most cases easier to accommodate. There is always less confrontation when all the cards are on the table. It's harder to handle a termination of employment than it is just not to take someone on in the first place, if it's not the right fit for either party. Don't take a punt or follow your gut feeling on someone - it rarely works out in the long run and real, focused recruitment policies can help galvanise the process.

The recruitment journey itself is discussed in more detail in a later chapter, but here are some additional tips for getting your people motivated, often with very little expense. This can become your bible and not to be missed by leaders when you are preparing to motivate their teams.

i.   Provide a great environment to work in – no one wants to work in a drab, run-down office. A bit of colour here and there, a lick of paint and a few plants can easily transform a dull environment into a positive one. If this seems an expense, then get the staff involved with the renovations of the office. You will be surprised by the boost in morale, and the involvement will build pride in the long-term care of the working environment.

ii. Employees will appreciate well-maintained toilets, kitchens and filtered water. 360-degree feedback has proved this point.

iii. Acknowledge an employee's achievement when they have a great result, gone beyond the call of duty or done something special within the business. The best way to praise someone is in front of their peers, but you could also see them individually. Always make sure it's face to face though – an email just doesn't have the same impact. We all love a pat on the back – it's a childhood instinct, but it still means a lot.

iv. Give your employees the right tools to be able to do their jobs well. Nothing demotivates employees more than not having what they need to do their jobs. It may be updating their computer, fresh training (either internal or external), support, even something as simple as a chair that doesn't wobble.

vi. Provide incentive schemes when targets are hit - healthy competition between departments can help keep morale up and focus on the job in hand. This is not just for sales roles and is easily emulated in many departments.

vii. Make sure you listen to your employees. You can't help them or change things if you don't know about the problems in the first place. Regular reviews and informal chats are essential. The motivation this interaction will give them can be huge.

Those are just a few examples of ways making your people happy, all very easy to implement. Unhappy people are not productive. If you don't address their unhappiness now, it could mean significant expense for you later, either through an inefficient workforce or high staff turnover. Either way you will lose the people you need to move the company forward.

Motivating people to do what they don't want to do

Now this is a different scenario altogether, and will often occur in even the most effectively managed situations. It's a great management challenge which most leaders will face. How can you persuade others without alienating them?

Imagine you're a manager in a major sales organisation and one of your teams fails to present an important element of the next big campaign. This is going to create frustrations, taking you straight back to the 'Black Line of Doom'. But instead of raging and asking irrational and ineffective questions, try the following two seemingly simple questions:

1. How ready are you to make the presentation, on a scale from 1 to 10, where 1 means not ready at all and 10 means totally ready?

   In the unlikely event that they say 1, surprise them by saying, 'What would it take to turn it into a 2?' In telling you the answer, they reveal what they need to do before they are able to make the presentation of work. That is what you motivate them to do first. To get to step 2, as a leader you check and re-inspect. This is vital and a personal mantra of mine. Never assume things are done and then ask this to be confirmed at the last minute. You need to set mini deadlines leading up to the major deadline - this way you can ensure an outcome that more likely matches your own. You have to remember that people will never do things exactly as you would as a leader. If you allow them to do the majority of the task, even if it's only 70%, you are not taking the task on, only maybe adding some valuable final touches. They will learn from the experience and get better at it. If you take the job away from them entirely and do it yourself it is almost like self-destruction; the result will be demotivation and increasing your own workload unnecessarily.

2. If they pick a number higher than 2, ask, 'Why didn't you pick a lower (yes, lower) number?'

Question 1 seems irrational, because you're asking, 'How ready are you...?' of a person who just said no, which we can assume means not at all ready. However, most resistant people have some motivation that they keep from us. If you ask, 'Are you going to take my suggestion, yes or no?' they continue to keep their motivation hidden. But if you ask them the 1-10 question, they're much more likely to reveal their motivation by saying 2 or 3, which is far better because you've now moved from a 'No' to at least a 'Maybe.' Try it, at least a few times - you will find it supports good behaviours.

Question 2 seems quite left field. However, by asking it, you're asking them to defend why your directive to present the business issue is even the slightest bit important to them rather than give their excuses as to why it hasn't be done (eg too busy). The answers they give lead to rehearsing the positive and intrinsic reasons for doing what you asked, which in turn dramatically increases the chance that they will actually get the project done.

Commissions and bonuses

So now we look at motivating people on commission, bonuses, kickbacks, or whatever you wish to call them - the murky world of motivating by monetary incentives. So far we have covered the relatively inexpensive issues of motivation through understanding your people as people. Now good salespeople can be different animals – yes, all the above still applies, but the expectation is different. People come into these roles expecting to earn as much as possible. Really target-driven people live for their commissions, which means these incentives must be key drivers for them. Target-driven people are those you come across by chance when recruiting, or perhaps they feel they have hit a ceiling in their current position, so in essence they find you. Remembering this during the recruitment stage is important, because the best target-driven people don't leave roles they are good at! If they are bringing in the business, the company they are working for will not want them to leave.

Put yourself in this position. You have a high-achieving sales person in your business who is making money. Wouldn't you do anything you can to keep that person in your business? I hope so, because if a sales person is achieving this means the business is generating new business which is converted into turnover.

So the pay structure can be key. This element of motivating, maintaining and driving employees through their pay structures, known to many as pay plans, can set the tone for how people perform within a business, and in my humble opinion it is used far too little. By identifying the key drivers of your teams, pay plans can be used to get the extra mile you may need to take your business to the next level.

Often pay plans are seen as plans for sales people only, but this can be very short-sighted. Every business requires a set of objectives to push people onwards. The reward for them may only be small, but a small incentive now could help to achieve improved profitability in the future.

5

DEVELOPING PAY PLANS

The key to successful pay plans is identifying what the business needs and mapping this to key performance indicators, or KPIs, for those individuals. We have already focused on understanding what has worked well for these types of people at the interview stage - knowing how they have been successful in the past works wonders in developing further improvement within your organisation. This has to be synchronised with your profitability goals.

Successful plans which should be considered include:

i.   Profit/gross margin (GM)

For many organisations the traditional method of motivating sales people is working with the margins they make on the deals they do. The £10k rule is always a good start - a £10,000 target per month per sales person. This is a good margin for generating good profit for the business and gives a real level of achievement for the individual. For example, if someone makes the business £10,000 of new sales per month they would be rewarded with a percentage of this amount. This could begin at 10-12.5%, which equates to an additional £12,000 to £15,000 per annum on top of whatever basic salary is agreed. For anyone this is a nice base on which to begin building.

ii.   The Accelerator

On top of this you can have levels of accumulative accelerators. To further incentivise after achieving the base profit targets, a good platform is to have levels of increasing bonus after the initial £10,000 target. By doing this you can continue to drive the individual to grow further each month, for example if they hit £12,000 the percentage increases to 15%, and when they hit £20,000 it increases to 20%.

These are just examples, but they begin to build a picture of how a pay plan can encourage over-performance month in month out. It avoids the problem of 'sandbagging', whereby employees save deals to enable them to hit the next month's target rather than putting the business in now to avoid missing out on valuable commission. This is a real risk for businesses which are too profit conscious. If people are making money for the business they deserve to see some of that in return, or face demotivation through seeing profits consumed by greedy owners.

Revenue targets

One of the down sides of profit or GM-based approaches is obvious: you have to have a wealth of trust in the people you employ, because they will realise just how much money they are making for you. This can be unnerving for many businesses, which may feel they are showing too much of the business to their teams. A good way to keep monetary-based targets without showing the profit/commission values to the employees is to use a very similar percentage-based model but focus on the revenue geared by a deal rather than the profit it actually produces. The same principals can be used in terms of percentage increments on revenue, but these have to be tailored to the specific business sector and a percentage that is viable. A little more thought needs to go into this model.

For example, if your deals are high value in terms of revenue say £1m total deal value more detail needs to be understood because by issuing a high percentage on these sales can leave you diluting much of the actual profit created from these type of deals. Internally within the senior management team (SMT) you are still working on a profit arrangement but you are simply not making the profit amounts clear to the sales team.

Continuing this example, if on a £1m deal only £50,000 profit is actually made for the firm because it is, for example, a reseller of products, then the overall percentage must reflect this so as not to give away too much of the business's profit to the sales staff. In this case the figure could be as little as 0.5%, which equates to a £5000 bonus - a huge incentive, but only 10% of the actual profit the business makes.

Productivity targets

This is a relatively new approach, but one I have found to be very fruitful in certain campaign-based industries, especially marketing agencies and the like. This is the requirement not to target against £££s of profit/revenue but against the productivity which will lead to these in the end. For example the targets are based on:

■ Number of meetings in a month with key people of influence.

■ Number of networking events that contains your key client demographic in a month.

■ Number of proposals sent to businesses in month.

Leaders may find the productivity approach quite dubious as you are very much running on assumptions, but in each environment where I have seen this approach it has worked. People are focused on the root causes of sales rather than the pressure of achieving a figure month by month, and over a year the opportunities for development are huge. Linked to this is the motivation of the individual themselves, who feels more responsibility, as the focus is on the work involved to get the sale. It becomes altogether a more enjoyable process, improving motivation to achieve.

These are just some of the ways you can use pay plans as a documented route to motivation though achievement within your teams.

As many leaders will know motivation is not always based on financial gain and can essentially be linked to much simpler measures. These may work better if you operate in different sectors, where the sales functions are not so defined.

Let's outline ways of recognising individuals by utilising both formal and informal rewards. They can be used for everything from a quick pat on the back for a job well done to recognition of individual or group efforts that have made a significant contribution to achieving company objectives.

'Pat on the back' awards:

i. Send the employee a recognition email.

ii. CEO or other high-level executive to thank the employee in person.

iii. Hold up an applause sign at the next staff meeting after you mention your employee's successes.

iv. Send out a weekly or monthly 'Great Achievement E-mail Award' to the entire company, acknowledging one outstanding employee.

v. Award the employee with a 'plum assignment' - their choice of what they want to work on for their next project.

vi. Send flowers to one of the less recognised 'behind the scenes' individuals.

vii. Create a 'Hall of Fame' in the reception area. Put up a picture of each employee of the month, and engrave their name on a master plaque with words of recognition.

viii. Hand out a 'Bright Ideas' award for innovative thinking. The winner could get a free dinner or tickets to a show.

ix. Give a 'High Five' award. Pick five people in the department and have them go up to an employee and say 'I heard that you did a great job at . . . Good work!'

x. Give a 'Mint Condition' award at the end of the year to all who had perfect attendance.

xi. Offer employees something that complements their favourite pastime (tennis lessons, golf club membership, cinema). This should have been ascertained at the recruitment stage.

xii. Pay for your employee to use a local car wash and get a tank full of petrol. Then there is a another tier for higher-level employees linked to high profit focus awards. These incentives need to relate to the fees generated by the individuals.

Outstanding/above and beyond awards:

i. Give out the 'Golden *** (symbol of your company or department)' award, to be passed from one outstanding employee of the month to the next.

ii. After an employee has finished a project involving long hours at the office, send their significant other a letter of appreciation and a gift certificate for two at a restaurant.

iii. Hold a monthly 'Queen/King of the Hill' day where the outstanding employee is given the closest parking spot, treated to lunch and let off early - or even a duvet day (a favourite, I have found).

iv. Pay for the employee and a friend/partner to go to a local restaurant, offering them the 'Above and Beyond' award for extra-long hours on the job.

v. Offer a 'Squeaky Clean Quality Service Award' where one outstanding employee has delivered quality service.

vi. Award a 'Lean and Mean' award for cost-effective work within or under the expected budget. Give the recipient a three-month membership to the nearest gym.

vii. Give an employee the 'Gracefully Handled' award when

they help the company pull through a sticky situation. Offer tickets for two.

viii. Give an employee the 'Golden Research Award' for detailed research they conducted to make a project successful. Offer them a subscription to their magazine of choice.

These can be over and above the pay plans already discussed. Remember that the more you incentivise the more the business will generate. The failure is to see this as wasting money – yet the risk is about what will happen if you don't do it.

As you will no doubt observe, the above are suggestions only - all need to be specific to your staff group and based on what you know about them by understanding these desires and interests. This is why personal profiles of your employees are so important. If you know what they do and what their interests are, you have a better model on which to motivate your teams. There is a lot in this list and certainly using all of them would be overkill (far too much management time), but some of these ideas should spark the creativity to come up with your own specific motivations.

EXERCISE

Take this opportunity to note some ideas down. Identify some which begin to align with the core values we have put together from earlier chapters. This exercise will also highlight how well you really know your teams.

A good exercise is to review your own motivational incentives - if you have not been using them, maybe you require them now.

Rewards can come in all shapes and sizes. The key is to

ascertain what works for each employee. I believe motivational profiles of your employees are just as important as the skills profile you create. An ideal time to gain this information is again during the interview process, and this will be explored in later chapters when we look at the recruitment journey.

It is wise to remember that not all motivation is down to the management hierarchy. It can be put squarely at the employees' door. However hard we try as business owners there will always be issues with employees themselves, as attitudes are hard to judge, and in later sections of the book we will address the issue of sounding this out at the recruitment stage.

It is vital to judge what people will be capable of once they are employed within the business. Management can't beat themselves up and blame everything on the hierarchy; put simply, people can just not be right for the culture you want to achieve. However, understanding what your culture is in the first place will help create a criteria for employees moving forward.

It will help to organise your management team to understand what to look out for within the existing staff group to ensure people can be put into categories which are effectively managed. A good exercise is to make sure you understand this before your next recruitment drive.

Here you can look at some groups and try to place existing employees into a group, identifying where they sit. If you have people in any of these areas or show the related traits, I would suggest they need to be addressed during your next appraisal or performance review to ensure you can work to a point where you either dispel the attitudes or remove the people entirely.

If you want to make sure you're providing your

employees with an environment in which they can thrive, check your workplace for these motivation killers:

Toxic people. If you've ever spent time with truly toxic people, you know how destructive and exhausting they can be. Toxic people spread negativity and suffocate the positive. Let them find a new home or if that's not possible, make sure policies and supervision are in place to minimise their damage.

Lack of professional development. Everyone needs to feel that they are learning and growing. Without that, the workplace grows static and dull. Professional development for each of your employees allows them to grow in their careers and to know that both the organisation and you have an investment in their success.

Lack of vision. A clearly communicated vision sets direction and lets people know where to focus. Without it, even the best employees are less effective, because it's hard to excel if you don't understand the big picture.

Wasted time. If you have the kind of workplace where meetings are called for no real reason and there's a constant stream of irrelevant emails sent to everyone, it's likely that your workers are deeply frustrated. Show people you value them by showing them you value their time.

Inadequate communication. When communication is poor, people spend half their time second-guessing what they're doing. Critical tasks are missed, nonessential jobs are duplicated, information is locked into silos and destructive rumours thrive. A clear flow of communication benefits everyone.

Vertical management. If you can remember being in a situation where your ideas and input weren't valued or even heard, where it was 'keep quiet and do what I say,' you know how hard it is to do anything more than a grudging minimum. The more collaboration, the more investment and the more motivation.

Lack of appreciation. When hard work or extraordinary results go unrecognised, when even everyday thanks are unexpressed, people grow uninspired and apathetic. You can reward your employees without spending a dime; it can be as simple as saying 'thank you.'

Bad leadership. Bad leaders harm every member of the team and every member of the organisation. Even the best employees need effective leadership to excel. Start by developing your own leadership, then hire and develop the best leaders at every level. It's the best thing you can do to improve your workplace for everyone.

If you recognise any of these motivation killers in your workplace, don't worry - if you didn't I would wonder why you have chosen to read this book. It's up to you to do everything in your power to become part of the solution. Remember, great people do not stay long in bad workplaces, which means more risk and cost to the business in trying to replace them or building a new culture from scratch. Leaving it too long may mean you have no business at all.

6

Key Performance Indicators

If you were to eavesdrop on just about any management or executive meeting, strategy session or performance review in any business, you would hear the term 'KPI' mentioned many times in many different contexts. Most people in those discussions would know that it stands for 'key performance indicators', but if you pressed each person to explain what a KPI actually is, it's likely that you would hear many different definitions.

Business is challenging, especially during difficult economic times. It is also extremely competitive, and our customers are becoming increasingly discerning. As a result business leaders and senior executives are all looking to improve performance, minimise errors and seek out new ways to gain the edge over their competition. KPIs, when properly understood and used effectively, provide a powerful tool in achieving that.

For those wishing to separate the rhetoric and flavour-of-the-month management fad approach from the genuinely useful information, check out *Key Performance Indicators for Dummies* on Amazon.

KPIs are ubiquitous in modern business. They are everywhere. And yet businesses which are using KPIs correctly and effectively are not common. Knowing about KPIs and understanding their relevance is of course important, but when push comes to shove KPIs are only really useful if you identify the right ones to measure for *your* business and only measure those. They will only deliver mission-critical data if you then use the KPIs, and analyse what they tell you on a regular basis to inform and illuminate your decision-making.

In simple terms KPIs help organisations understand how well they are performing in relation to their strategic goals and objectives. In the broadest sense, a KPI provides vital performance information that enables organisations or their stakeholders to understand whether the organisation is on track towards its stated objectives or not. In addition KPIs serve to reduce the complex nature of organisational performance to a small, manageable number of key indicators which provide evidence that can in turn assist decision making and ultimately improve performance.

If you think about it, this is the same logical approach we use in our daily lives. Say you are not feeling very well and decide to visit your local doctor. He may ask you what is wrong, but he's immediately searching for evidence to qualify your subjective opinion. He may for example take your blood pressure and measure your cholesterol level, heart rate and body mass index as key indicators of your health. With KPIs we are trying to do the same in our organisations. Without them we are flying blind, relying on the often subjective assessment and opinions of key personnel.

In practice, the term KPI is overused and misunderstood. Too often KPIs are assumed to be financial or numerical only, yet this definition is much too narrow. KPIs do not just describe any form of measurement data and performance metrics used to measure business performance; they are anything that indicates a difference between one thing and another. If you can observe a move from one state, situation or element of performance to another that is strategically or operationally important to the success of your business, then you can measure it. And that measurement is a KPI.

Unfortunately there is often a disconnect between whether something can be measured and whether it should be measured. Instead of clearly identifying the information needs and then carefully designing the most appropriate indicators to assess performance, KPIs are too often implemented using what is sometimes referred to as the 'ICE'...

■ Identify everything that is easy to measure and count.

■ Collect and report the data on everything that is easy to measure and count.

■ End up scratching your head thinking, 'What on earth does this all mean, and what are we going to do with all these numbers?'

Starting with the data that does or could exist is a recipe for disaster and will have you disappearing down data dead ends, wasting valuable time and money. Just because you could figure out how old your customers are does not mean you should. Just because you can assess the time between orders doesn't mean you should. When it comes to KPIs, always figure out what it is you need to know first and then design the KPIs to deliver the answers.

7

SELF-MOTIVATION

To follow on from the previous chapter, you have to understand that there will be a level of self-motivation with your teams, and harnessing this early will be a key route towards developing your people. According to *Psychology Today*, motivation is literally 'the desire to do things.' Therefore, self-motivation may be described as 'the initiative to begin or continue an activity without any external influence'.

Unfortunately, our motivation is easily affected by circumstances and predispositions, as we have clearly indicated in the previous section. Changes in motivation can result in unfinished tasks, unfulfilled goals and even apathy about a job, a relationship or life itself. How then can we guard against a loss of self-motivation and keep the fires burning to drive achievement and success?

Below are six elements which can help support self-motivation among your teams, something that as a leader you can install in your teams:

i. **Purpose:** We are essentially custom-made - handcrafted in a way. Therefore, you have significant, eternal value. Your purpose is found first in the One who ordains your life and every step you take. You have been gifted with talent and have much to offer the world and the people you influence. True motivation comes from knowing your purpose and the destiny He designed exclusively for you. *'When you find your definitions in God, you find the very purpose for which you were created.'* – Dr Ravi Zacharias.

ii. **Peace:** Everyone fails. Get over it. Make peace with your past mistakes and failures. Learn from them, but don't let them hold you back. Too often, we give up trying for fear of failing, and lose motivation. Let it go, and keep moving forward. *'I have not failed. I've just found 10,000 ways that won't work.'* - Thomas Edison.

iii. **Perception:** A positive self-perception leads to optimism – the fuel required for action and achievement. Avoid over-inflating or undervaluing your capabilities. Both can cause a loss of motivation, because false self-perceptions lead to challenges with projects getting started, quality, deadlines, deliverables, etc. Instead, use sober judgment (and a coach or mentor) to objectively assess your strengths and limits *'You cannot consistently perform in a manner which is inconsistent with the way you see yourself.'* - Zig Ziglar.

iv. **Positivity:** In order to maintain an optimistic outlook, set mental and emotional boundaries as guards against pessimism. When negative or self-defeating thoughts enter your mind, move them out quickly, lest they lead to self-sabotage. *'No pessimist ever discovered the secrets of the stars, or sailed to an uncharted land, or opened a new heaven to the human spirit.'* - Helen Keller.

v. **Prudence:** Regarded as an ancient virtue, prudence is *careful good judgment to govern and discipline oneself by the use of reason.* Thomas Aquinas said that prudence starts with the 'act of inquiry.' To get the outcomes you want, take the time to do your homework. Read. Learn. Research. Grow. Avoid impulsive thoughts, words and actions, which typically lead to undesirable outcomes, resulting in loss of motivation. *'We must believe what is good and true about the prophets, that they were sages, that they did understand what proceeded from their mouths, and that they bore prudence on their lips.'* – Origen.

vi. **Progress:** Finding an answer. Completing a task. Achieving a goal. Each of these stimulates a strong positive emotional response within us. Even solving the simplest problems will kindle your motivation to achieve more. So always track your achievements and draw energy from them when times are tough. *'Of all the positive events that influence inner work life, the single most powerful is progress in meaningful work.'* - Professor Teresa Amabile.

Motivation is a very big topic and many excellent books have been written about motivating and self-motivating. These are just some thoughts on the subject which have certainly worked for me. To begin, start slowly and work your way through each of these six pillars, exploring how to apply them based on your circumstances, as every business is different. The introduction of models helps get past the worry of doing it in the first place.

8

THE NOTION OF PRODUCTIVITY

What is productivity - really? One thing is clear – it's most certainly different for every organisation. Productivity is a sweeping statement about what your business is doing and how effective it is. It's mentioned in management meetings every week, but I have seen first-hand how it's become an idea rather than a measurable statistic in management. Each employee's output should be measurable, so productivity has to be measurable. Management information systems (MIS) need to be in place in order to validate productivity and create effective workforces.

MIS is seen as a big word and possibly only available in the corporate world. Like the values myth discussed later, MIS can be developed in all business formats and you should begin simply by looking at accounts, output and revenue to determine where in the business the key drivers for success are. As a guide I have selected two businesses I am actively involved in and I will discuss how they use MIS to measure productivity. They are very different sectors involving very different outputs, which means the MIS focus is different, but it still offers the same value.

Telecommunications sector (sales). Measurement of productivity in:

i.   Number of outbound calls per day.

ii. Sales figures vs commissions targets.

iii. Gross margin of a proportion of sales generated (GM).

iv. Campaign activity - what calls are made to what target audience and why?

v.   Number of clients visited.

The list can become exhaustive, but hopefully you see the pattern - pretty generic for a sales department.

The private healthcare sector

i.   Measurement of productivity of a private care home business

ii. Occupancy rates - number of available capacity of a period of time eg 3-6 months.

iii. Staff turnover/staff ratios - number of staff leaving in a set period.

iv. Shift hours/work patterns - number of hours required to work and number of shifts.

v.   Cost of delivery of care - The break-even point per client to deliver services.

vi. Margin per week per person, after cost is considered.

The second sector is not so obvious as in the direct sales arena or transactional business, but still very palatable, and enables the leaders/managers to make decisions about the business by accessing this information. All too often these are not considered. In every industry there is a level of MIS which can be accessed to understand better the performance of your people in their given task, always linking back to the main business goals. This will help drive improved productivity with a measured approach.

All businesses should build a productivity model and do an analysis of what their employees do and how they add value to the business. This will not only help to identify the measurable output of employees but help evaluate whether you are a high-value producer or a great-efficiency producer. We all want maximum income for minimum output - this is Utopia - but how much do we truly know about the people we employee vs the income they contribute to produce? By identifying high fee earners and non-fee earners through this process you will improve managerial expectation of individuals based on their income value to the business. This is not to say some people are worth more than others, but it gives a clearer reflection of where the concentrated development is needed to increase the likelihood of further successes in the future.

If your business does not already do something similar, or it is not a business-as-usual function, I suggest you put this book down now, go to your calendar and pencil in a session with your senior teams to discuss this, regardless of what industry you're in. Just try it. Make a decision on measurement of productivity and trial maintaining this. Over a period of time your understanding of what employees achieve will be much clearer, undoubtedly changing your focus or maybe helping to develop changes to pay plans to reflect the roles people are actually playing within the business. Constant monitoring of this is then vital for you to measure it further — it's not a one-time only task but becomes the norm.

9

Boosting your productivity

Once you establish the measure for productivity, this needs to be discussed with employees in a way that makes people buy into your new model. There are many ways to motivate, as discussed, and it's not all down to the management. People can make their own improvements to productivity with encouragement. Here is a variety of simple techniques. I'm sure you all have your own ideas, but here are a few you can try:

i. Get a boost. Research has stated that people are less likely to make decisions after lunch, so by providing a boost to people with potassium (a banana is best) as part of FREE fruit available in the office will help this process.

ii. Sleep - encourage people to get rest. Making employees work through lunch and late in the evenings is less

48

productive in the long run. Encourage them to take a break and rest in the evenings - this will mean you get more done during business hours. This is surely better motivation for everyone than long hours in the evening with no lunch breaks. You will have seen the adverse effects if this happens in your firm.

iii. New-wave thinking. As with everything now, there is an app for that! Encourage your employees to source applications which support their working life balance. Rescue Time is a great tool for helping support procrastination and Headspace, which promotes mindfulness, is another good support. This takes the pressure off management and leaves the support mechanism firmly with the people. I have personally been using rescuetime.com for a while – it's like a personal trainer highlighting your web surfing weaknesses.

iv. Outsourcing tasks. Not only CEOs can outsource. Encourage people to outsource workload which they feel is hampering performance, and ensure senior members have junior people who can take on non-productive tasks. This may be the role of an apprentice, discussed in a later section. The initial outlay will always be worth more long term.

v. Encourage organisational skills by helping your people to engage with tools which promote improvements in this area. Understanding tasks which are to be achieved in a day, joined with a measured level of importance, drastically improves an individual's productiveness. I still run a daily to-do list in Evernote (an application available to all at evernote.com), which has tasks labelled with level of importance to me. I grade them A to E - an A task is high priority, whereas an E task is not so. Another useful way to denote priority could be a pound sign system, often used in my sales days, £££ High, ££ Medium £ Low, or whatever suits. The key for this is to understand that all tasks must be achieved, but some days they will not all be completed, so it's best to understand which ones are worth more than the others and must be done first and best.

vi. Introduction of a timetable. A daily schedule is useful for each department - what are you actually doing and when? Clearly indicating to people when tasks are to be achieved can breed great behaviours in the workplace, building a better culture. An example I have used for telesales is as follows:

Time Frame	Tasks
8.30am	Admin - check emails and set a to do list for the day with priorities.
	Set calling objectives for the day based on what happened on previous shift.
9.00am	Daily briefing with sales leader.
9.30am	Start daily calling.
	Callbacks from old leads followed by lead generation for new business.
12.00 to 1.00pm	Begin second admin period - send out quotes from morning calling.
	Access emails.
1.00pm to 2.00pm	Take a break from screen and work - go to lunch, mix with teams.
2.00pm	Begin afternoon calling and check to-do list - chase any quotes sent which are due for today.

4.30pm	End day's calling - final admin - check emails again for any business.
5.30pm	Finish for the day.

The above table seems simple enough, but it provides focus on some major work-related points which are often ignored. This is a clear indication of what someone needs to do in a day. Not only does it clearly identify that admin tasks should only be done over a two-hour period, it offers a substantial break period and does not require anyone to stay late working unsociable hours. Defining times enables people to be very clear and achieve their set objectives. For instance, four hours of the day is allocated to outbound calling, purely focused on business hours when people are available to talk to. However it clearly shows that any paperwork related to this calling is saved for outside this time, because the time spent on this detracts from the real job of creating new business opportunities.

The clear objective here is to carry out the work required within achievable time periods. This is the true goal, as more often than not lack of productivity comes from a lack of understanding of what is important and when. So helping your teams to increase this understanding simplifies their work processes and brings increased productivity, and in most cases better employee-to-employer relationships.

Although there may be no perfect answer to the people v performance v productivity conundrum, there is one approach that is fundamental for profitability: get the right people in the right roles working on the things that matter most to the business.

10

PERSONALITIES, AND HOW TO MANAGE THEM

Running a business would be easy if only you didn't have to manage people. How often have you thought that, or joked about it? Of course, you need people to run every aspect of a business. The bigger your company grows, the less the likelihood that everyone in it will be easy to supervise. As the boss you always (or almost always) have the option to let anyone who is truly a drag on your company go. But good talent is hard to find, so before you go down that road, it's worth the effort of trying and make a difficult person work more effectively within your company.

When faced with a problem personality, most of us do one of two things. We either confront the person head on, which will always lead to escalating hostility, or avoid dealing with him or her altogether, leaving the problem to get worse. Neither is an effective solution, and as your company's leader, neither is an option.

There's a better way, according to Judith Orloff MD, author of *The Ecstasy of Surrender*. Instead of being rigid and laying down the law, you can use a sort of 'communication aikido' to channel troublesome employees' own energies in ways that will benefit them, their co-workers and your company.

People typically react when their buttons get pushed. If that happens to you, take a break, breathe and centre yourself. Then respond calmly and firmly, rather than getting caught up in their dances. As a role model for others, you have to be in a higher place. From the helicopter view, as I have always put it, you will undoubtedly feel the wrath of frustration, but this must be kept to the confines of your own office.

Here's a look at five of the most challenging personalities we have all encountered at some point, and how to manage them effectively.

Narcissists

Narcissists have an inflated sense of their own importance and crave constant attention and praise. They're self-absorbed and lack the capacity for empathy. You have to realise that this person won't care what other people are feeling, which is a huge drawback in the workplace. Telling someone how their behaviour is making others feel, or working to the detriment of the company - an effective approach with many employees - won't work at all when you're dealing with a narcissist. Narcissists are also extremely sensitive to criticism of any kind and liable to react badly to it. If you want to keep them on and be productive, you have to frame a suggestion in terms of how it might serve them. That's the only thing they'll respond to.

What's a good role for a narcissist? Interestingly, they will often do well in positions of power, because they take that power very seriously and value it highly, and often work very hard in those roles. Narcissists are running the world!

Passive-aggressive types

These people will promise to help you with a project, but then they don't. Or they'll show up 15 minutes late. Passive-aggressiveness is a form of anger, but not an overt form. You may be tempted to try and get to the bottom of what's making them angry and try to resolve the problem. Don't go there, It's a character disorder. You have to dig very deep.

Another thing to watch out for is your own reaction to passive-aggressive people. These people will leave you dangling. They can make you feel you're not worthwhile because they don't show up for you in a consistent way. They can get to you without you knowing it.

How do you deal with passive-aggressive employees? Unlike narcissists, they do have the capacity for empathy. They also want to advance in your workplace, and you can use both these traits to help motivate them. Mainly, Orloff says, you have to set very, very clear expectations. The only way is to say very clearly what you need from them and when. 'It's very important that you show up on time for our meetings,' for example. Chances are they'll try to slip through any loophole they can find, so you have to be very precise about what you want them to do.

Not surprisingly, passive-aggressive employees work best in jobs where there are very specific guidelines and expectations laid out for them. In more open-ended roles, they'll drive everyone crazy.

Gossips

Every workplace will have a certain amount of gossiping, but if one of your employees enjoys reporting bad news about you, others in your company or even the competition, that's destructive behaviour and you need to do something about it.

The first step toward dealing with a gossip is not to get sucked in yourself. Don't participate in gossiping, which can be hard to resist, depending on the subject of the conversation. Even more important, don't give in to the natural human desire to know exactly what's being said about you, or to try to please everyone so they'll only have good things to say.

Beyond that, it's a good idea to call the gossip on his or her behaviour, and explain that it's not helpful for your workplace. Bringing their attention to it will curtail it a bit. It's good to do this because if you don't, it will go on unchecked. Beyond that, Orloff advises talking about gossip and its destructive effect to the company in general. 'The workplace is a breeding ground for gossip,' she says. If you address it honestly and explain why it's not good for your company, you give employees permission to tell people that they don't want to participate in gossip.

On the plus side, gossips often have good people skills; they like talking, so if you give them a positive place where they can talk, you can channel their abilities for the good, Maybe sales is a good role.

Anger addicts

Some people deal with workplace tensions by accusing their co-workers of misdeeds, yelling at others and generally giving their angry feelings free rein. These are some of the most challenging employees you'll have to deal with. Whatever you do, don't let them get away with it. This is unacceptable behaviour, and this situation needs intervention. They have to be given very strong limits and boundaries. It will destroy a workplace if people are having tantrums.

As the leader or manager, you'll either have to take anger addicts aside, or get someone in Human Resources to do so. Either way, they need to hear that their expressions of anger are inappropriate. Offer them the opportunity to go for counselling. And face the fact that anger addicts may not have a future at your company, since repeated rages can potentially drag your whole organisation down.

Guilt trippers

Guilt trippers lay it on thick. If you gave a plum assignment or perk to someone else, or otherwise slighted them or made their work more difficult, they'll let you know just how much of a grievance they have. They may lay the same guilt trip on co-workers who they feel have slighted them as well.

With guilt trippers, educate them on how to communicate better. A guilt tripper doesn't know anything about communication, using the word I - 'I feel this way' - rather than 'You did this to me.' Just a little education about that might help. You can also talk to them about the effect their comments are having, since guilt trippers often don't realise how they're affecting others.

What's the best role for a guilt tripper? Not with people. Have them work on independent projects.

As with all external views, each has to be attributed to the scenario at hand. It's good to research outside the box when it comes to behaviours in the workplace. Some of the points raised here may seem a little over the top, but if you step back from your business and look at the personality traits discussed you will be able to see where people may fit on this scale and how this could be affecting business productivity.

Hopefully this will help you to engage with some of the people within your organisation, or if not at least to know what to look out for in the future when developing people in your business.

11

STATE, NOT SLATE

The good news followed by the bad news finishing up with the good news, or a favourite phrase of mine, the 'shit sandwich'. This term reflects the process when discussing business-related topics direct with employees on a professional level. This could be about performance, attitude or worse, a more sensitive issue, which should all be handled with the same care.

If you're not in a calm frame of mind, don't entertain this for any reason - nothing good will come of that scenario. The key is to start by avoiding the fatal mistake of saying 'Don't take it personally'. Really? You're talking to, let me check... yes, it's a person. You're talking about them, their work, their livelihood, their ideas, their sense of competence, their choices, their discretionary effort, their life's work etc and then you're telling them not to take it personally? If the shoe was on the other foot how would you react? This is a defensive start and won't bring about a happy, controlled meeting environment, therefore failing to motivate either party.

How about you do this as an approach. Give every person who works for you a free pass for a week to make whatever comments they like to your face about what you say, do, or suggest, in whatever terms they wish, so long as they preface it with 'Don't take this personally'. If you don't think the act of working with others is in any way 'personal', perhaps you might be better thinking of a career as, I don't know, a beekeeper, maybe? Bees really don't take things personally, or so I have heard.

The idea of dealing with employees directly is an emotive part of management and many pitfalls can arise, but the key is to listen and take in what the employee has to say before offering a full response.

Unfortunately many situations where a one-on-one discussion is necessary will relate to an issue, a problem or a criticism. As touched on in the introduction, public dressing downs will do nothing to solve any situation nor improve overall morale. So there are many advantages to private engagement with employees on these matters.

Private criticism

No employee is perfect - we all know that, and nor are we, as leader/managers. Every employee needs constructive feedback on what they are producing for your business. When they are following key guidelines or tasks this is even more necessary, to ensure they are on schedule for completion. Also employees deserve constructive feedback in their work, whatever the response to that is. All too often we see where feedback is not provided, whether it be good or bad, because if it's good there seems to be no need to praise and if it's bad the first thought is to bury our heads in the sand and hope it improves. Newsflash -neither will benefit you or your teams. Good managers give that feedback, and great managers always do it in private.

Public praise

This follows on from the motivation points we discussed. Every employee, even a relatively poor performer, does *something* well. Every employee deserves praise and appreciation. It's easy to recognise your best employees because they're consistently doing great things. (Maybe consistent recognition is the reason they're your best employees? Something to think about.)

You might have to work hard to find reasons to recognise an employee who simply meets standards, but that's okay: a few words of recognition, especially public recognition, may be the nudge an average performer needs to start becoming a great one.

So why a shit sandwich? It's about the management of the interaction, giving both praise and feedback at the same time, and can be a great system for employee communications. Good, bad, good, positive comments followed by effective feedback and topped off with some more positives - it works every time and makes an employee listen to the feedback in the middle as they are motivated by your previous contributions to the discussion. Taking the option to give just negative feedback is unhealthy and rarely brings a single positive outcome.

For most business owners, changing your culture from fearful to honest and open could be seen as not only daunting but almost impossible, but this need not be the case. For many businesses it should be the start of building plans for motivation within the workforce. Open and expressive cultures are the way forward, as demonstrated by fast-growing companies across the world. If you research the growth of SMEs in the UK, they all have a vibrant, expressive culture with a flat hierarchy which breeds creativity.

Some approaches to help you move away from the fear factor and begin building staff-focused cultures are:

i.   **Put your ego to one side.** It's difficult, as previously suggested, for some leaders to incorporate this into their working life, but is absolutely essential. The idea of surrounding yourself as a leader with 'yes' men will only lead to developing your ego rather than gaining honest feedback on your performance and the company's. This is a brave approach, but required. True leadership must come with the ability to take on board development points, even from your employees. This feedback needs to be embraced and used for further development. Refusal to even take on board this feedback will mean putting further distance between leaders and theirs teams.

ii. **Encourage openness.** This is a key element in engaging with employees. They want to feel part of the company, and many meetings have surely passed when people were bursting to make a comment or full of ideas but were afraid to. This is not what you want - this initiative will go elsewhere if not encouraged. The leaders themselves must encourage open discussions, as this then breeds the right culture from within.

iii. **Embrace employees publicly.** To enable employees to talk openly and offer ideas, there has to be a forum in which they can feel comfortable in offering up these thoughts. There have to be avenues created for employees to make these responses. Not all will find comfort in doing so in a meeting environment, certainly not when the approach is first introduced. Try a suggestions box - 'Ask the boss' - on an intranet or newsletter, with an open invitation for email dialogue. All will show a willingness to listen to employees' commentary, breeding fluid conversations between them and yourselves as leaders.

iv. **Ignite the fire**. Once you have a more comfortable environment there may be a need to push the boundaries with more information to hand as a leader with the introduction of the feedback, and harder questions can be asked of the business. Leaders can begin to ask more thought-provoking questions about the business with greater expectation for responses which will drive it to new successes.

When looking at whether you are a 'state not slate' business in terms of management style you tread a thin line, with the danger of bullying. There is a high level of risk, as it creates a sense of demotivation with an organisation; there is a narrow divide between good management and harassment. With the increase in employee support externally a key leadership skill must be to differentiate between being direct and bullying individuals. People's emotions can take control, leading to a breakdown in communication, and this can have a catastrophic effect on the working relationship between personalities.

The table below, taken from www.bullyonline.org, can help you recognise a bully in the ranks. It's a good benchmark against which you can monitor yourself and your managers to see whether there is a bullying culture within the organisation. This poses one of the highest risks, as it can damage your business, your productivity and essentially your profitability.

A TRUE MANAGER	AN UNDERLYING BULLY
Leader	Bully, coward
Decisive	Random, impulsive
Has a good appreciation of short, medium and long-term needs, goals and strategy	Rigidly short-term, often no more than 24 hours
Accepts responsibility	Abdicates responsibility
Shares credit	Plagiarises, takes all the credit
Acknowledges failings	Denies failings, always blames others
Learns from experience and applies knowledge gained from experience to improve business, communication, language and interpersonal skills	Has a learning blindness, cannot apply knowledge gained from experience except how to be more devious, manipulative, and how to better evade accountability
Consistent	Inconsistent, random, impulsive
Fair, treats all equally	Inconsistent, always critical, singles people out, shows favouritism
Respectful and considerate	Disrespectful and inconsiderate

Seeks and retains people who are more knowledgeable and experienced than self	Favours weaker employees, recruits henchmen and toadying types
Values others	Unable to value, constantly devalues others
Includes everyone	Includes and excludes people selectively
Leads by example	Dominates, sets a poor example
Truthful	Economical, uses distortion and fabrication
Confident	Insecure, arrogant

An exhaustive list is available, but this gives a flavour of the most obvious traits.

It's important to evaluate yourself and your managers against this profile. It may sound like a strange request, but understanding these issues early is the best way of solving the long-term problems that will arise with regard to the turnover of your staff. Always remember that the most costly part of any business is the employees and what it costs to constantly replace them when they leave. So don't give them a reason to leave in the first place.

Don't look at this list and think, that's not me. I know it's difficult not to look at this list negatively, but do be honest in your thoughts. Hopefully the fact that you are still reading this book indicates there is some opportunity to grow and develop as a leader to enhance your business. You can help engage with the rest of the management on how to create a plan of change which ensures these traits do not continue or occur at all, thereby beginning to mitigate the risk of it happening at all.

Few employers understand how a bully impairs productivity, hinders performance and damages profitability. Let's look at a typical example of the effect of one serial bully on one department's performance.

Population of the UK: 60,000,000.

Number of workers/employees: 28,000,000.

The majority of advice line cases involve a manager bullying a subordinate in a professional or semi-professional context.

The average wage for a lower-middle level manager or professional is around £20,000 pa.

The effect of bullying on a targeted subordinate is to cut their work rate and effectiveness by 50% (at least), therefore the annual cost of bullying to the employer in this department is £10,000.

The serial bully impairs the effectiveness of other employees, so say a further four employees earning £15,000 pa have their performance impaired by 33% (4 x £5000), plus a further eight employees earning £10,000 pa have their effectiveness cut by 20%, ie 8 x £2000 = £16,000.

Target:	£10,000
+4*£5000:	£20,000
+8*£2000:	£16,000
	——-
	£46,000

Experience from over 10,000 bullyingonline.org cases suggests that these estimates are in fact conservative.

The majority of bullying is carried out by a superior, so let's say the bullying manager is a grade higher, on a salary of £25,000 pa or above. The serial bully is a dead weight who survives by plagiarising other peoples' work, so his/her annual cost is £25,000. Although glib and plausible, only when the serial bully leaves will it be really discovered how little work that actual person has completed - and much of that will be to a poor standard, requiring the work to be scrapped or done again properly.

Serial bully:	£25,000
Effect on employees:	£46,000
	——
	£71,000

This is an astonishing amount. It may not reflect what is going on in your business now, but what if it occurred and the damage it created was not picked up until it was too late? The lowest estimate of bullying, according to a CIPD survey, was that 1 in 8 workers are bullied each year, which equates to around 3.5 million people in the workplace right now.

Let's not forget that this doesn't include consequential costs, legal costs, insurance costs, compensation costs, staff turnover costs, re-recruitment and re-training costs, loss of investment in training and experience, loss of employee potential, benefit costs, injury to health, loss of revenue due to employee being out of work and no longer paying tax, family breakdown, costs to society, etc.

This is surely a risk worth avoiding. Finding further ways to reward staff will enable you to create a successful profile for your business, reducing the risk of these incidents. All business processes have a cost of failure/nonfulfillment, so successful monitoring of the workforce removes this concern.

There was a lot in that, so I'll summarise what this means to you as an employer:

The bully is not fulfilling his or her duties and obligations but is consuming salary; the bully survives by stealing other people's work and the credit for it.

The bully is preventing other members of staff from fulfilling their duties; over time, staff will spend more and more time covering their backs and less and less time fulfilling their duties.

The bully is the main, but least recognised, cause of negative stress in the organisation. The divisive, disruptive and dysfunctional behaviour of a serial bully can spread throughout the organisation like a cancer.

Replacement cost: the cost of replacing one employee is at least £5,000 for advertising and basic recruitment costs, plus an amount approximately equivalent to the employee's annual salary while that person gets to grips with the job, learns procedures, makes contacts, builds networks, etc. Some estimates put the induction and retraining cost at three times annual salary.

Is it worth the damage to your business NOT to evaluate and find out what is happening within your teams right now? As with many elements throughout, take this opportunity to make some notes on any of the teams or individuals where these points begin to ring true. Make a note to document a time to work through this with any individuals as a priority task for you as a leader of your business.

Remember - 'Never push a loyal person to the point where they no longer care'.

12

THE CULTURE, OR STRUCTURE

Common values

Many businesses talk of 'values'. This is sometimes an over-used word, especially in the corporate world, with many businesses happy to spend millions of pounds developing key words which they believe will forge a culture the business will be proud of. This is all well and good, but as with anything there is a need for user involvement - because if you want values to have an impact you need to find out what they will impact, who they will affect and how. The only people who can help with that are exactly the people who are working for your business.

Values can create a real springboard for actions with a business. They can install a sense of belonging, which is clearly good for all involved, as everyone seeks belonging in areas of their lives and it is no different in their workplace.

Few things create greater trauma than doing something

that doesn't match what we value as people and as a business. Many large corporations promote core values and use them to create training programmes, development schemes and recruitment plans; there is a reason why time is invested in these ideals. This doesn't mean SMEs cannot adopt such approaches. I have found that the introduction of values that map the business and its people can have a profound effect on the long-term relationship between the business, its owners and ultimately its employees. Values set the direction of people's behaviour.

One way SMEs can approach the introduction of core values is to begin by picking three things they as the leader or manager value most. It might be pride, or sincerity, or faith, or family, or cooperation, or adventure, or camaraderie, or humility, or independence - the list is endless. A task I believe to be essential for a senior management team is to pick three of these values and then see which of them work for both your business life and family life.

Then ask your teams to do the same thing - pick three values. In a team, briefly launch the news that the business is now looking to introduce core business values to shape the business. From this exercise you will almost create a whiteboard session of all the possible values for your business, and they will almost become more focused. They may include:

- Trust
- Pride
- Service
- Knowledge
- Quality

- Communication
- People
- Fun
- Market
- Innovation
- Caring

Involve the whole business, whatever size it is, to brainstorm the values. This will open your eyes to how the business is perceived internally. Again the list could become almost exhaustive. Further involving the teams in creating the common values of the business will bring togetherness within the company. Their involvement in the creation of the values can ensure that they are more likely to become embedded within the workforce, bringing further empowerment. Please do make this an exercise for your business, because you will see the improvement immediately from those who see the value in the involvement.

The final part of the exercise is to narrow the values to just a few, maybe four to six - whatever suits - and finally to ask the company to vote for the one they prefer. The overall consensus will offer up the final values that the business can take forward. These values should then be laminated and put on display around the premises. Why? Because this makes these values visual, not only for the existing teams but for new employees who join the company and for those clients who come to your offices. If people are low, a bit lost or lacking motivation - which will happen from time to time despite what is being achieved - these values can be used to self-motivate acting as a reminder that everyone is part of the business's growth.

Although many companies have nice-sounding value statements already featuring such concepts as Integrity, Communication, Respect, Excellence etc, this doesn't mean they have done anything for the organisation itself. They may be displayed in reception or on the walls, but they cannot be real core values of the business when they are just selected by senior teams and left for everyone in the business to follow. The actual company values, as opposed to the nice-sounding ones, are shown by who gets rewarded, promoted or even let go. Actual company values are the behaviours and skills that are valued in fellow employees.

The rise of fast-growth organisations who have really adopted values are open for all to see. Take Netflix as an example - this massive online streaming media service business in the US adopts nine values, which are as follows:

Judgement

You make wise decisions (people, technical, business, and creative) despite ambiguity.

You identify root causes, and get beyond treating symptoms.

You think strategically, and can articulate what you are, and are not, trying to do.

You smartly separate what must be done well now, and what can be improved later.

Communication

You listen well, instead of reacting fast, so you can better understand.

You are concise and articulate in speech and writing.

You treat people with respect independent of their status

or disagreement with you.

You maintain calm poise in stressful situations.

Impact

You accomplish amazing amounts of important work.

You demonstrate consistently strong performance so colleagues can rely upon you.

You focus on great results rather than on process.

You exhibit bias-to-action, and avoid analysis-paralysis.

Curiosity

You learn rapidly and eagerly.

You seek to understand our strategy, market, customers, and suppliers.

You are broadly knowledgeable about business, technology and entertainment.

You contribute effectively outside your specialty.

Innovation

You conceptualise issues to discover practical solutions to hard problems.

You challenge prevailing assumptions when warranted, and suggest better approaches.

You create new ideas that prove useful.

You keep us nimble by minimising complexity and finding time to simplify.

Courage

You say what you think, even if it is controversial.

You make tough decisions without agonising.

You take smart risks.

You question actions inconsistent with our values.

Passion

You inspire others with your thirst for excellence.

You care intensely about Netflix's success.

You celebrate wins.

You are tenacious.

Honesty

You are known for candour and directness.

You are non-political when you disagree with others.

You only say things about fellow employees you will say to their face.

You are quick to admit mistakes.

Selflessness

You seek what is best for Netflix, rather than best for yourself or your group.

You are ego-less when searching for the best ideas.

You make time to help colleagues.

You share information openly and proactively.

These culture focus points were published in 2012. They could be seen as an exhaustive list for some businesses, especially start-ups, but the premise is important. It is people focused, it's evolving and it wants its people to buy into it, but the values have been developed from the type of people already in the organisation and what has helped the company become what it is today. These values are the same throughout the organisation as it goes from strength to strength, and Netflix is not afraid to say that if you don't fit this ideal, then working for them is probably not for you. This is clearly mitigating the risk of underperformance, followed by setting really strong expectations of its employees present and future.

Many examples of this approach can be found in other fast-growth businesses. It's not hard to find out what they are doing that makes them great by doing a little research. More often than not it is the establishing value-based relationships the company has with its employees - very powerful stuff when done right.

13

ENTREPRENEURIAL HIERARCHY

Although we have been looking at entrepreneurial ideas, that isn't what this book is about – it's about the people you employ and how they are treated. Although the entrepreneurial business models with fast growth endeavours are the future, hence why many such as Netflix already mentioned have enjoyed such short-term success, the mind-set with regard to employees has changed dramatically. This includes looking at the hierarchy of a business; the new model for hierarchy is much flatter, negating the necessity to employ in positions where people are not needed.

Business structure and the culture within is an interesting double act. The culture is the end goal, but the structure is the building blocks that can aid the development of culture as a blueprint for what you stand for as a business. Different authors describe culture as a complex pattern of shared behaviours that distinguishes people from each other and is transmitted over time.

Those who can't follow structure are everywhere in business, and they are sadly usually at the top; as with much of the tone throughout, the key is not a wishy-washy approach but an understanding of what your business actually is and what its culture is. There is no strict rule for how this is performed, as many cultures especially within the most entrepreneurial ventures, are born out of the passion and drive of the originator. The type of people who are drawn to start-ups are independent self-starters anyway who thrive on uncertainty - think about it, they would have to be, wouldn't they, to work in an unknown environment? That's great, except when you're trying to get them to follow your lead. Here are a few ideas for leading people like this without resentment or unnecessary rules.

What's the biggest risk facing the leaders of most entrepreneurial ventures? It's not closing that first round of funding or landing a cornerstone customer. As with most things, it all comes back to people, and your ability to lead those who don't have much practice following. In turn you might not have much practice at leading, so it's time to learn, and fast.

It's easy to get seduced by the investors, the technology, the contracts and the customers. It's even easier to focus on those things when you don't want to take on the challenge of leading a green team. But in the end, it's your people who hold the fate of your venture in their hands, and leading them well may be the most important work you do.

Whether you earned your stripes in a corporate leadership environment or as a serial entrepreneur, you carry many embedded assumptions about the way people should follow their leaders. Unfortunately, no one has explained that to the members of your team. That's your job. You have to teach them how to be good followers and team members.

It's not about hierarchy

Most of your team members are part of your entrepreneurial venture because they enjoy the absence of excessive structure and bureaucracy. Try to teach the art of following by enforcing a rigid structure and you will have taken the first step towards killing your company culture. Instead of explaining the organisational chart (trust me, everyone already knows it), help them to understand the power of directing every team member's creativity, hard work and determination toward a few key goals. Explain that it's your job to set that direction, monitor the course and get them everything they need (money, people, resources etc) to move the organisation toward its destination. Be sure to emphasise that their job is to accomplish the tasks along that path as described earlier.

It's not a democracy or a true meritocracy

Many entrepreneurs hold egalitarian management ideas. 'The best idea wins!' we proclaim. Unfortunately, the best idea is not always practical or pragmatic. In that case, it falls to the leader (you) to squash it, which can inspire more than a little backlash from its most passionate supporters. So be careful in the expectations you set and assumptions you allow when canvassing your organisation for good ideas. Additionally, remember that incentives aren't always aligned. We discussed incentives in a previous chapter and here is where they can be mapped effectively. Younger salaried employees have very different goals from founders or executives with a personal investment whose compensation hinges on the performance of the business. Those incentives lead people to assess decisions very differently, and it may lead your people toward projects that are at odds with your goals. You set a tone with your decision-making style. Set the wrong tone and you'll either never make a decision or your employees will grow frustrated when their recommendations are overridden. Simply explain the major constraints (time, money, technology, etc) and how the decision will be made (democratically, by a committee, by you with input from others). Once the decision is made, be sure to explain why that path was chosen. Transparency helps your team see how you're keeping the organisation on track with the goals you've previously articulated.

Help them to be better followers

By explaining that your role is to set direction, provide resources and drive decisions, you'll help your newer team members understand how they fit into that broader organisational picture. Failure to do these things will result in frustration, disillusionment and gridlock. The better you're able to teach your people to follow you, the farther along your desired path you'll go. There is nothing more time-sapping than answering questions which could be set out from the very start.

People prefer a pecking order

Yes, people actually do prefer a hierarchical management structure. A structure of some kind breeds disciplined people; it also makes the company look like it knows what it's doing.

As with many aspects you have to look at both sides. Not all businesses are in their entrepreneurial stage; without doubt more mature business need hierarchy. Maybe it's not such a good idea to banish the organisational chart completely, because a recent study by Stanford Graduate School reveals that many employees secretly like them. If you've ever been part of a bureaucratic organisation, you know how frustrating it can be to deal with several chains of command, which makes getting things done quickly all but impossible. That's why start-ups often champion 'flat' organisations and do away with unnecessary levels of management as a way to stay fast and nimble.

Although you might not be doing your employees (or your company) a favour by eliminating chains of command altogether. A great saying I heard at an event one year from a successful female entrepreneur was 'Better to have a hole than an arsehole'. A brash statement yes, but very accurate. The issue with too formal a hierarchy is that you end up recruiting for recruiting's sake to fill a role, which is not the way to do it. Later in the recruitment journey we look at the better developments in this area to irradiate poor recruits.

There are real benefits to a hierarchy for many reasons, which actually include motivating the very workforce it serves.

In a hierarchy, it quickly becomes apparent who gets access to whom, which positions are coveted because they come with better pay and status, and so forth. Take away all the levels and things get more interesting, albeit more confusing. Equality can be messy, and hierarchy is conceptually cleaner. That's not to say hierarchy is always better than equality in the workplace. In fact, plenty of companies use an egalitarian structure to foster unique environments in which workers are more free to innovate. This is ever more prevalent now with the offices of the future in the tech world which so dominate social media, giving high expectations for workforces which are seen as behind the curve.

How to strike a balance

Although there may be successes in a business with a flat structure, this comes with some association to a more formal hierarchal approach. People often think equality is a natural state that doesn't have to be managed, but it does. Isn't it harder for people to understand and learn when the structure is so undefined? So you need more clarity in other structural variables, like job titles, for instance. Spelling out relationships among staff is another way to help employees understand how an organisation works. This leads to clearly define roles and responsibilities.

So, should you throw away the organisational chart? Not unless you're ready to give your employees the kind of clarity they will need to thrive in a flatter organisation.

14

THE CULTURE TOOLKIT

'We're proud of what we do round here – we all want great outcomes.'

We all know from discussions here and in other text that workplace cultures influence the working environment, driving the quality of the service provided and the results that are achieved. We also know that positive workplace cultures have a profound effect on how staff feel about their work, how they behave, what they achieve and even how long they stay in their posts.

Positive workplace cultures do not just appear. They need to be developed and maintained in order to provide a better understanding of organisational culture and its significant impact on performance. Some areas for consideration when re-engaging with a culture are considered below.

1: A sense of identity

People who work within positive workplace cultures are more likely to benefit from a united sense of identity and a feeling of belonging. This can encourage loyalty to the employer and collaborative team working. The commitment to work together is of particular value where staff work alone or in pairs, but need to work as part of a wider team to ensure continuity of a culture.

2: Shared values and assumptions

Values are of particular importance within organisations, as discussed in Chapter 1. The values within positive workplace cultures closely align; they will be values such as openness, trust, integrity and respect. Whilst it is essential to recruit people who have the right values to work in your specific sector, it is also necessary to continue to develop these values through investing time and energy into maintaining your positive workplace culture. If workers are themselves made to feel valued and treated fairly with dignity and respect, they are much more likely to treat those they work with and clients they work for in a similar manner. Failure to nurture either staff or organisational values is likely to have significant consequences for the quality of the service delivered.

3: Norms and expectations

Many sectors are continually under pressure to develop high-quality services that deliver flexible and personalised client support. In such times of change, positive workplace cultures encourage and support people to improve the service they deliver. Norms and expectations are key aspects of workplace cultures and have a significant impact on how people behave over time. In positive cultures, they can support staff in becoming confident and capable workers, responsible for their own learning of new skills through qualifications and other continuous professional development opportunities. There are clear expectations of how people will behave towards each other and those they support. As a consequence, individuals feel more able to speak out about practices or behaviours they have concerns about.

4: Lines of communication

Open and transparent communication is a vital element in a positive workplace culture. Whether you are talking to your clients about the service offering, discussing an individual's plans, agreeing appraisal outcomes with a member of staff or writing the business plan, every act of communication must be clear and understandable. Jargon, acronyms and other practices that potentially exclude the uninitiated must be avoided.

Of course, communication goes far beyond the spoken word. Attention must also be given to how people communicate in non-verbal ways. Clear communication is also essential where teams are widespread, based over several sites or where members are lone workers. Good internal communication, role modelled by leaders and managers, will also set the standard for staff to copy in their interactions with others, including colleagues and professionals. However, every individual is personally responsible for the tone, content and the style of delivery of the communication.

5: Complex sub-cultures

Those leading the development of a positive culture should work to identify the positive and negative elements or influences within their workplace. These may be individuals or sub-cultures that have the potential to support or disrupt the achievement of the organisation's aims and objectives. Within some settings, sub-cultures may develop amongst different teams, maybe those working on night shifts, those who have different roles or staff who are recruited from different countries or for whom English may not be their first language. Larger organisations will probably have many sub-cultures as they have many teams within many different departments. Individual employers may also find sub-cultures within their team, even when they only employ several PAs. Leaders and managers will need to address the negative and build on the positive attributes of these sub-cultures so that they are aligned with the organisational aims and objectives.

6: Continuous change and development

There are many demands on a workforce, particularly the need to evolve services that are flexible and tailored to clients' requirements. The increasing demand for better value-for-money services in all sectors can be a key driver for these developments. The slow-changing nature of workplace cultures can support the process of positive change, whether this change is from choice or necessity.

Over time, cultures will inevitably respond to internal and external influences, and skilled leaders and managers can steer this process to achieve identified, desired outcomes. Well-led, positive workplace cultures are also flexible, responsive and resilient; these characteristics are particularly useful when rapid changes are required in response to unforeseen circumstances. However, it is important to realise that leaders will rarely have control over all factors; it can be hard knowing how best to lead change, and employers may find that some successes may be achieved more by luck than design! These challenges can be mitigated by an ongoing awareness of the elements of a workplace culture, and careful monitoring of both positive and negative developments.

These six areas can be used to help design any culture change programme and can act as a toolkit for redevelopment, even if this is just to check where you are at and more importantly what you are actually doing at all. With so many items to consider it is very important to ascertain where you are in terms of culture, as they can be created over time with little input from anyone. The entrepreneurial hierarchy scenario talked about earlier in the chapter shows clear examples of this happening. A worthwhile exercise is to ask yourself, your managers and your staff (those who want to of course) where you and what you think can be done to improve the current culture.

By having a six-area benchmark you can begin by analysing these areas and creating a culture review process. You can take a simple scale of each area and gain an understanding of what areas are working and how they could possibly be improved to cope with future pressures the business will face in years to come.

Culture Assessment Tool

AREA	5 Excellent	4 Very good	3 Good	2 Poor	1 Very poor
A sense of identity					
Shared values and assumptions					
Norms and expectations					
Lines of communication					
Complex sub-cultures					
Continuous change and development					

The above Culture Assessment Tool, as adapted from Skills For Care UK and the Kings Fund, will enable you to show where these areas are currently from a solid perspective within the organisation. It will give a baseline to build from and from which to assess progress. Once it has been completed you can then devise actions to help improve each stage and review in 6-9 months' time to see how these developments have gone. The hope is that each area will be moving closer to the 5 and not backwards towards a 1. Even if it's the latter, at least you are aware of it by having measurement in place, something that is often forgotten in organisations. Remember, measurement is everything. How can you fix, improve or progress when you don't truly know where you are within this section of your business?

15

THE HEDGEHOG CONCEPT

I have always found it very useful in any process, including culture, to congratulate yourself sometimes - pat yourself on the back and say 'this is what I'm good at!' In other words, identify your organisation's 'hedgehog' - what it is that you do better than anything else.

The 'hedgehog' concept was devised by Jim Collins, who in his book *Good to Great* uses the parable of the clever, devious fox and the simple hedgehog. The fox keeps coming up with new ideas to eat the hedgehog, but the hedgehog handily defeats him by doing his one trick: rolling into a spiky ball. This idea is now used widely in organisational development. The hedgehog concept highlights the importance of organisations knowing what they're good at and keeping strategies simple, pursuing them with drive and determination.

To identify your workplace 'hedgehog', along with the other activities discussed, work with your colleagues to identify answers to the following questions from the circles below.

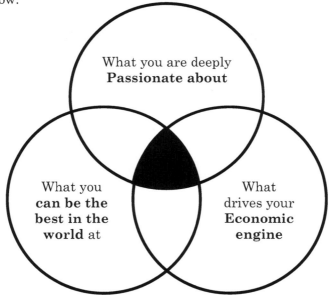

The greyed area in the centre of the three circles is the 'hedgehog'.

- What do we, as leaders and workforce, care passionately about? Most people work best when they believe in and are committed to the service they are providing, so it is important to identify what these things are.

- What do we do well? (And equally important—what we do not do well). This may be small scale or very focused, for example it could relate to how you support people to use assisted living technology, how you ensure mealtimes are a positive and dignified experience for all, or maybe you have a great induction for new staff.

- What are our drivers?

- How do you measure success?

You might include factors such as reputation, financial profit, workforce health and wellbeing or customer satisfaction. Once you have the answers to these questions (and you may have several answers for each one), consider the diagram below, focusing on where the circles intersect in the middle. Identify what answer fits in this intersection. It must address all three questions - you must be passionate about it, do it well and it must be one of the factors that drive your business. This is the activity that you can work as a business to deliver time and time again. By understanding what it is, you can begin to build your values and core recruitment structure around it, and it defines the major milestones of your business.

Achieving the 'hedgehog' will also support your positive workplace culture. It creates opportunities for people to work together to identify strengths within the service (and possibly each other) and then to jointly plan how to build on this. This encourages people to commit to delivering the 'thing they do best', and to have a sense of shared identity and pride in its achievement.

An example: using 'My Care Services Business', the scenario from shared values and assumptions, my workforce might answer the three questions in this way:

What do we, the workforce, care passionately about?

- Delivering innovative care solutions recruiting people with the right values.

What do we do well?

- We listen to people to hear their needs and wishes. We have strong links with the community leaders. We are supported to learn the skills we need.

What are our drivers?

- Having a business that has a strong value base delivering personalised care and support and having a good reputation, increasing the number of people we work with.

Our 'hedgehog' is developing specific community networks around individuals as they develop more independent lives, offering a rounded continuity of care provision.

After progressing the stages of your culture design, you will build the roadmap of the journey your organisation wants to take, although it is always good to remember that things will happen along the way that can affect the culture you have developed. These can come in the form of:

■ A new member of staff joining.

■ Poor feedback from your clients and service users.

■ Securing a new lucrative contract.

■ Winning a prestigious business award.

These are just some things you should have in the back of your mind, so when these things happen (which they will), you have a process for managing this within the culture. In a later chapter, when we look at the recruitment journey, this should help with ensuring this has little effect on a culture with a new employee, as you have to be firm. If the culture works don't recruit someone who will not fit it - this is will always fail.

16

THE LOYAL EMPLOYEE

Every small business or entrepreneur hopes to have loyal employees. Yet loyalty has absolutely nothing to do with length of employment. Recalling the previous sections, there are some real hot points which can help the understanding of what constitutes loyal employees and what to look out for.

Who is more loyal:

■ The 10-year employee who does just enough to get by, criticises you and your business at work and at home, and frequently and not-so-subtly undermines your decisions?

■ The six-month employee who genuinely embraces where you want to go and works hard every day to help you and your company succeed?

While experience does matter, I'll take the six-month employee every time. Loyal employees work hard for their pay and are committed to your company's success. They may one day leave, but while they work for you, they do their best and often even put the company's interests ahead of their own. Phenomenally loyal employees hit the next level. They aren't just loyal to the company, they're also loyal to *you,* even though their loyalty can be displayed in surprising ways.

Here's what the most loyal employees do:

They tell you what you least want to hear. As a general rule, the more rungs on the ladder that separate you and an employee, the less likely that employee will be to disagree with you. For example, your direct reports may sometimes take a different position or even tell you you're wrong. Their direct reports are much less likely to state a position other than yours. And entry-level employees will sing directly from the company songbook, at least when you're the audience.

Truly loyal employees know that you most need to hear what you least want to hear: that your ideas may not work, that your point of view is off, that you made a mistake. They'll tell you because they know that although you may not care much for what you hear, you care tremendously about doing what is best for your company and your employees.

They treat you like a person. Remember when you were in high school and you ran into your teacher at, say, the supermarket? It was weird. She wasn't supposed to *exist* outside school. You didn't see your teacher as someone who wore shorts and had friends and wore a band T-shirt and actually had a *life.* Your teacher wasn't a person; she was a *teacher.*

Lots of employees see you that way, too - they don't see you as someone with dreams and hopes, insecurities and fears. You're not a person; you're a *boss.*

Genuinely loyal employees flip the employer-employee relationship. They know you want to help them reach their professional and personal goals and that you want what's best for them - and they also want what's best for you, both at work and in your personal life. They see you as more than just a boss, and they treat you that way.

They never criticise you in front of others. 'Bash the boss' is a game almost every employee plays, at least occasionally. (One of your employees is probably talking about you right now.) Partly they criticize you because it's a way of letting off steam, but mostly they do it because we all think, at least some of the time, that we can do a better job than the person we work for. Criticism, mocking, sniping - when you're in charge, those things come with the territory.

They also chip away at the respect you work so hard to deserve. Loyal employees get that. They don't gossip, they don't snipe, they don't talk behind your back - they give you the respect they expect to receive themselves, even when you're not around.

They still disagree, but only in private. Debate is healthy. Disagreement is healthy. Weighing the pros and cons of a decision, playing devil's advocate, sharing opinions - every leader wants to hear what his or her team thinks. It's not just enlightening, it's stimulating.

Truly loyal employees trust that they can share their opinions as freely as you do. In fact, they trust that you *want* them to-because you and the company benefit from an honest exchange of differing opinions and points of view. But once a decision is made...

They totally support your decisions - and you - in public. I guarantee you've been in at least one meeting where someone says, 'Look, I don't think this is the right thing to do, but I've been told we're going to do it anyway. So let's at least give it our best shot.' After that little speech, does anyone ever give it their best shot? Even when they disagree with a decision, loyal employees don't try to prove you wrong. They do everything they can to prove you *right*.

They tell you when they need to leave. I've never known an incredibly loyal employee who wasn't also just a plain old incredible employee. Because of that, you want them to stay. You *need* them to stay. Still, sometimes they need to leave - for a better opportunity, a different lifestyle, to enter a new field, or to start their own business. But they also know their departure will create a tremendous hole, so they let you know what they're thinking to give you plenty of time to prepare. Granted, if an employee is willing to tell you well ahead of time that he or she is planning to leave, or is just thinking about leaving, it means they trust you to an exceptional degree. Clearly they know you won't start to treat them differently or fire them on the spot.

This employee trusts you because he or she's been loyal to you. After all, they have put their interests ahead of yours a number of times - and now they know you'll do the same for them. And if you won't, what kind of boss are you? The kind that doesn't deserve loyal employees. Be the kind of boss that earns loyalty because you are loyal not in return, but *first*.

17

The recruitment journey

The infamous JDs

So why is this journey so important, and why do so many businesses get it wrong? Sorry to say this, but it's true. I myself was a victim of poor recruitment, so I'm not just pointing the finger. The phrase 'square pegs in round holes' is old but very apt, even now. In all my years of teaching and consulting around workplace performance, I see three reasons why employees consistently underperform: they are incapable, they are disconnected or they are unclear.

Research shows that 51% of HR managers believe poor job descriptions can mislead employee expectations, resulting in them being a poor fit and ultimately driving them to leave. Moreover, 68% say poor job descriptions contribute to weak candidate pools and 59% believe they result in wasted time with irrelevant candidates who have the wrong skills. *(Taken from People Management - monthly CIPD Magazine 2014.)*

1. **Employees who are incapable**. These employees have core abilities that do not align with the abilities required to complete the activities of the job. Every job has very specific activities that are key to performance and therefore to success in the job. For example, the activities of an accountant are to close the accounts, create reports, analyse performance, ensure compliance with procedures, etc. These activities require a strategic, analytical, methodical and detail-oriented person. If your accountant employee is not that, performance is a challenge. Many times the primary reason for employee underperformance is hiring employees who do not fit their role – they do not have the abilities that align to the specific needs of the job. Solution: Include the required abilities in addition to skill and experience criteria when defining the performance profile of the job; hire for abilities as well as skill and experience.

2. **Employees are disconnected**. These people do not share or understand the direction, vision, belief or mission for the business; there is no emotional connection to the business. When employees understand the beliefs and vision of the business and they align with their personal values, they are more engaged, committed and passionate about their performance. Think of the way employees at Google feel about innovation, the way employees at Starbucks feel about coffee, the way employees at Patagonia feel about the outdoors. Our performance is fuelled by our passions and values – and diminished by lack of interest or connection. Solution: clearly share your vision and belief about the business and source/hire employees who share your beliefs.

3. **Employees who are unclear**. These employees do not understand their specific performance expectations. They don't know what a successful or 'done right' outcome is; they have no performance standard. Here is a personal example: when my kids were younger it seemed we were always in conflict with them about keeping their rooms clean. The problem was, we didn't share the same definition of 'clean room.' So once the room was cleaned 'at expectation,' we took a picture – then taped it to the door. This became the standard for how a room was to look when we said 'clean.' We all shared the same expectation or standard and now could hold the children accountable for delivering it. In the workplace, employees need the same guidance about what a successful performance outcome is so that they can be held accountable for delivering it. This clarity lets them use their abilities to determine how to deliver the outcome. Solution: improve the clarity of performance expectations to ensure employees know what is expected and can perform accordingly.

Sustainably high performance requires that employees' abilities fit the activities required of the job, share the values, beliefs or mission of the business and clearly know their performance expectations. We can't expect employees to bring their A-game if we haven't set them up to be successful. Once in place, it is fair to expect great performance.

The infamous JDs

Lack of clarity when it comes to job descriptions is demotivating for individuals, and affects engagement and loyalty to the organisation. This has a knock-on effect for teams, which are much more likely to perform when each member has an accurate picture of their role. On average, one third of UK organisations experience annual staff turnover rates above 21%. This comes at a significant cost to many. Staff turnover is costing companies with 100-249 employees over £138,000 per year (CIPD UK Survey 2014).

HR managers in the retail, engineering and legal sectors, in particular, identified a strong relationship between poor job descriptions and greater staff turnover. In the retail sector, 67% of respondents said a poor job description leads to mismatched job expectations, causing employees to become unhappy and leave. 60% of HR managers in the engineering sector believed badly-written job descriptions result in poor consistency and quality across the business. Meanwhile, 83% of HR managers in the legal sector said poor job descriptions affect existing employees as the wrong talent is brought into the organisation.

Get job descriptions wrong and there's a risk you'll recruit the wrong people. Get them right, however, and you can attract the best candidates, people who know what to expect from the role and how to make an impact.

86% of UK HR managers surveyed by CIPD said good job descriptions lead to better quality candidates. However, 42% believe that the quality of job descriptions drafted in their organisations are poor and over three quarters (79%) agreed that getting good job descriptions from managers is time consuming.

Every company in the UK can improve employee retention and team effectiveness by getting job descriptions right. But managers often don't know where to start. Give them the tools they need, such as Hay Group's Job Description web application, and empower line managers to create the right job descriptions, while HR maintains oversight. This not only speeds up the process but means managers, and the business, are using tried and tested information expertise on competencies and job evaluation.

Many of you will be used to the constant requests from recruitment agencies for the infamous job description. I remember that early in my management career I used to be frustrated at being asked for such a document - why was I being asked for something that they should know already? I have had a conversation with them and told them what they are looking for, can't they just get on with it? And then when they send me a CV or personal profile from this type of interaction, guess what - I didn't like the person. Why?

The issue is, I didn't understand what I was really looking for in terms of a person, a member of the team. Understanding some of the factors already discussed throughout helps create a more focused requirement of employees only helping to further improve recruitment.

Start with this question. Think as an employee and ask, do I know my job? Sounds obvious, but is it? Many people understand the roaming brief of a position but rarely undertake the true essence of what they are supposed to be doing. In one of my businesses in 2011 we took steps to further develop our supervision process, as we had found that various areas of training were not down to having to retrain but just getting people to think on their feet more. So one of these tasks was simply named 'My Job as a....?' We found from this exercise that even people with the same job came up with different answers, highlighting a lack of understanding. The main issue with lack of understanding is not a fault of the employee but a fault of the management structure for not defining the job role more clearly to each individual, whether they are existing employees or more importantly, new recruits.

So going back to the discussion of job descriptions or roles and responsibilities, if you so wish to call them these, they are vital to all within the hierarchal system to enable to differentiate clearly who does what and when. Therefore these documents should be clearly defined objectives, leaving little room for confusion. You benefit greatly from doing this at the recruitment stage, for many reasons:

i.   You get the right people.

ii.   Less time spent between yourselves and an agency.

iii. Better equipped people for interviews.

iv.   More focused people from day one.

An example of a job description used for a care management role within one of my businesses would have looked as follows. Use as you will, because all the aspects are clear and concise and can be used in all forms of employment. The key part is the deliverables. By being clear about the role, you set the expectations at the point of employment.

Figure: Job Description Example
Job Title: Care Home Manager
Accountable to: Directors
Responsibilities:

1.   To ensure overall compliance of the home to appropriate legislation, regulations and local registration authority guidelines. In addition CQC Regulations under new standards and RIDDOR.

2.   To keep abreast of all new legislation, regulations and local authority guidelines and to ensure effective communication to all staff.

3.   To plan, organise and conduct staff meetings.

4.   To set out disciplinary rules in consultation with senior staff and to

ensure that such rules are applied consistently and fairly to all employees.

5. To ensure that the fabric of the home and all attendant installations, equipment and appliances are maintained to the highest order in accordance with health and safety requirements, in liaison with directors.

6. To arrange planned maintenance/servicing/calibration as appropriate and/or repair installations, equipment and appliances, in liaison with directors.

7. Attend service installations and equipment installations.

8. To maintain the list of preferred suppliers and sub-contractors to the home, and to ensure that this list is regularly reviewed through management meetings with the directors.

9. To monitor stock levels of consumables and to order items as may be required, all items and requests to be agreed with directors.

10. To calculate staff hours weekly and pass on to the accounts department. Within this, to ensure monitoring of sick and absenteeism of staff on a monthly basis, forwarding the information to the operations director.

The idea of a job description above shows some key points and key roles that the job holder will be responsible for undertaking while in post, this list can essentially be endless and in a way should be as long as you need it to be. These expectations are set along with a clear line of development, as they are tasks, which are undertaken as actual measurement of delivery with this particular employee. This may seem a long-winded approach – for example the Job Description used in my own Care Group for a manager has 28 points, but the development of such descriptions, linked to the common values of a business, goes a long way towards offering further rewards to the organisation long term. This is found in reduced costs and time spent on constantly recruiting, and it can become a working document for developments.

For example, colour coding. Green could mean priority parts of the role, attributes that must be shown immediately. Amber would become short-term goals, which can be monitored, in a probationary period in the role over 3 to 6 months of serving in the post. Finally red would be long-term goals, ideally linked to incentives such as a pay review or bonus schemes. This measurement works as a win-win for both parties. The employee gets what they want long term in return for ultimately what the employer wants as a business. Linking goals to recruitment embraces the set expectations of both parties, removing any possible ambiguity, a feeling I'm sure we have all felt during the recruitment process.

18

THE RECRUITMENT PROCESS

The interview process is an important step, one that is sadly underdeveloped in many instances; the recruiting of new employees is vital for the growth of the organisation, but it can bring disaster when not executed properly. Entrepreneurs regularly comment that when they start a business the difficulty is then growing it through introducing the right staff and key people in key roles.

Previously we looked at the values of a business. A value culture is important to ensure at the interview stage that new people will fit in. One of the biggest risks is recruiting the wrong people. This is expensive to sort out and ultimately time-consuming, taking you away from your daily activities, the priority activities, which will lead to your business goals. Failing to follow a consistent interview process becomes an increasing challenge, with daily demands and management schedule changes. When the process is not efficient and well thought out the process can drag on too long, so that it becomes almost impossible to remember the applicants, leading to poor recruitment decisions.

Organisations tend to interview differently. The common threads include sourcing some CVs, then one or two interviews followed by a decision. I'm sure this short suck-it-and-see method is familiar to everyone. In my experience, 95% of the time this is all that is done. As with everything in business, the less planning the poorer the outcome (we have all heard of the six Ps - Piss Poor Planning = Piss Poor Performance (excuse my language, but it's a simple and relevant statement) and recruitment is no different. It comes down to creating a system and processes, which reflect the rest of the business. If you have a clear system, all members of the current teams understand the requirement of new people and can follow this through.

It begins by having an actual structure of the business and knowing what roles are required, then each time someone is recruited it is because the system warrants it. Once you understand where they are needed the process of recruitment can begin. I always think there are two boxes for recruitment - a senior role specific to a department and an operational level task-orientated role. They will generally be recruited using the same processes, but a mindful eye is cast on the number of people interviewed for the roles. When looking at senior posts, be as specific as possible in narrowing down the search to key people, ensuring a more successful long-term employment.

Task-orientated recruitment: When recruiting for this type of role it is best achieved in three stages:

1: Telephone screen.

2: Assessment centre.

3: Formal final stage interview.

Putting yourself and the candidates through a three-stage process galvanises the recruitment, because this shows real commitment to the role, both from the employer and the potential candidate. It makes everyone involved feel valued, giving a great initial impression to the business because so much time is seen to be allocated to recruiting new people. This begins the value chain for your new recruits, and whether they come on board or not the message is sent back out into the marketplace that your business really cares for its staff. Because of this I have seen those who have failed the process initially keen to re-apply in 6-12 months' time following their initial stages of interview. Perception is so important.

For the business, the commitment of an applicant provides a useful indicator for their working life with you; if they can commit to a three-stage interview where different skills will be utilised, this shows they have the commitment to work with you long term. Let's be honest, anyone can turn up to a single interview and impress on the day with words of wisdom from past roles, but to turn up to three separate specific events means real commitment to work for you and your business.

The telephone screen: So why telephone-screen applicants? What value does this add to the process? I appreciate we are all busy, so this is a task that is easily delegated to team managers or HR team members, but it is a low-cost, low-time intensive approach which facilitates a better understanding of the candidate. Why waste time seeing someone based on a CV that has been skimmed over?

The investment of booking in time and carrying out a thorough interview should only be carried out with a properly-screened quality candidate. On the phone the values and drive of an individual can be assessed very early; sometimes the fact that they actually answer the phone is a start within itself. Schedule a time for the call - if they don't answer then the time wasted is minimal. Compared to holding a stage 1 interview which they may not show up for, phone screening is a much more time-effective approach - cutting the wheat from the chaff early in the process.

The assessment: Arranging assessment days can be seen as a huge effort, but again it will pay off in the long run. Having people in practical environments will bring out their true standards of work and show up what they will do in a workplace - surely much better than a suck it and see approach. It's a shame how few SMEs do anything like this, because once they are employed it is harder to performance manage people out of a business than it is to simply not recruit them in the first place. This is the true risk in recruitment.

Components of an assessment centre:

1. Presentation by the employer.
2. Group exercises (for example, case studies and presentations).
3. Individual exercises (for example aptitude tests and psychometric tests).
4. Interview (technical or competency).
5. Role play and simulation exercises.

Throughout the assessment centre you can assess on a score sheet. Usually one assessor is assigned to each candidate on each exercise, and they rotate through the day. At the end of the day the assessors discuss their opinions with each other to decide on scores. Each candidate at the assessment centre will be examined against their individual score sheet, and you will not get to see your scores; the assessors often complete it when you are out of the room. The score sheet will be matched to the set of competencies the business is looking for. These competencies will of course be born out of the values of the business. An engaged member will already have investigated these via your website or by looking round the office on arrival, as discussed in a previous section on common values.

Typical competencies are below. As you will see, these are very similar to our initial common values.

1. Communication
2. Teamwork
3. Leadership
4. Customer focus
5. Influencing
6. Problem solving
7. Achieving results

The job description is the place to look to highlight what competencies you as the employer are scoring against during the assessment centre. Good candidates will home in on this and display this sense of awareness. Skills typically assessed at the assessment centre are communication, interpersonal skills, leadership, negotiation and the 'fit' for the business. Obviously each assessment centre will be looking for a slightly different skill set depending on the job role.

Essential elements of assessment centres:

1. Predefined competencies (skills) against which candidates will be assessed.

2. Realistic simulation of the skills required for the role.

3. Fair and unbiased assessment, for example pooling of data from different members of your existing teams.

4. Standardised recording of behaviour, for example create a simple score sheet or at minimum a comments sheet alongside a copy of the CV.

Use the scoring sheet to highlight whether people have researched your business, your sector and even your competition, because an understanding of what you do and why you do it from an early start point will enable a more fluid induction into your teams.

With the invitation to attend an assessment centre, give details of the day and an overview of what you expect. This will include an itinerary, joining instructions, address etc. Conducting the assessment centre will need a lot of thought into the type of exercises you want to use, and the exercises should really be unique to your business. The bespoke nature of assessment centres means there is no set template they follow. However, below is an example of a typical one-day assessment centre.

10:00	Arrive, collect name badges, coffee etc.
10:15	Introductions and presentation by the employer this ideally is done by someone as senior as possible.
10:45	Verbal and numerical reasoning tests - these can be found online from examples such as stickypeople.com.
11:45	Personality questionnaire - Many examples available online.

12:30	Lunch with managers and current employees - this is optional of course.
13:30	Technical interview.
14:30	Refreshments.
14:45	Individual task: in-tray exercise.
16:00	Group task: case study exercise.
17:00	Debriefing and payment of travel expenses.
17:30	Departure.

Whilst the informal activities such as lunch and refreshments are not directly scored, you should use these as an opportunity to see how candidates socialise with other candidates and your employees. This will show people in a relaxed environment in readiness for the afternoon's more interactive activities, and the initiative here should not go unnoticed.

As you can see, the day is jam-packed. As much as monitoring performance in each exercise, you want to see how people perform under a heavy workload, as this will simulate a busy day in the real job.

There are many types of group exercise used at assessment centres. Group exercises at assessment centres involve measuring people's ability to work in a team, contribute, delegate and solve problems. You are looking for candidates who can listen to other people's ideas, be positive and articulate their own ideas. In short, measure the skills which are useful in a real working environment. Hopefully you can see why an assessment centre is more useful to your business than a simple interview; how else would they find out that if candidates have a worrying tendency to start sulking when colleagues disagree with them?

The case study exercise is a realistic simulation of the type of business or strategic problem they are likely to encounter in the new role (if they get the job!) Typical competencies assessed in the case study are:

- Analytical thinking
- Assimilation of information
- Commercial awareness
- Innovation
- Organising
- Decisiveness
- Judgement.

A case study example presents the candidate with a series of fictional documents such as company reports, a consultant's report, results from new product research etc. They will then be asked to make business decisions based on the information. This can be done as an individual exercise, or more likely done in a group discussion. I find this much more productive as it is more in line with the candidates' team-working ability.

After analysing the documents and deciding on a way forward, allow the teams to discuss. They will be required to present a proposal in the form of a brief report or presentation maybe, or a group discussion is quite suitable. With individual case studies, you could also ask the candidates to present your recommendations at an interview. The exercise is assessing their approach to solving problems as much as the solution they arrive at. In fact, case study exercises usually tend have one 'correct' answer. As long as you logically see justification in the recommendations and these stand up to interrogation, this is a good sign.

These assessment routines must be tailored to your organisation and scenarios linked to the role in which they are possibly going to be working. Failure to do this can result in less than informative outcomes. I suggest on the next round of recruitment required in your business you should take the opportunity to deliver a session in this way and see the outcome. If all the elements are well thought out, the conclusion will be an improved return on the time invested - I can guarantee it.

The interview: If you want candidates to feel passionate about your business, the interviews needs to be an exciting and positive experience which will set the tone for the business and their possible role in it. The best interviews are conversations, although it's hard to have a conversation when you ask a series of fairly unrelated questions. No matter how hard you try, the process will feel, to the candidate, more like an interrogation, and where interrogations are concerned, there are no winners.

So instead always look to ask good, compelling questions. Some examples I have researched for use myself are:

i.   'What single project or task would you consider your most significant accomplishment in your career to date?' Great question, but here's one I like even better, because it gets to the heart of every small-business owner's needs:

ii. 'What one skill do you possess that will most impact our bottom line?'

Right away with these two you find out if the candidate knows anything about your company. It's hard to say how you will influence the bottom line when you don't understand what truly drives value for a company. More important, you begin to get to the heart of the value the employee will provide - valuable information on whether his or her strengths truly meet your needs within a role. So why not ask these types of questions and then do what comes naturally: have a conversation?

A major point, yet something many entrepreneurs forget to do, is to listen to the candidate's answer. As a business leader the common wheelhouse is endless discussion of the business, but the candidate should have done enough research in preparation so that you shouldn't need to give too much. When I feel I have said enough about myself and my business, I remember this: 'When you talk you are only repeating what you know, when you listen you may learn something new'. Think about that each time you feel you are wandering into promotional territory. You must listen to what the candidate says, not just discuss the business or be thinking of the next question on your list. There should be no next question on your list. Simply think about what you just heard. Then ask a question you would ask if you had run into the candidate in a coffee shop.

I know you're thinking that might be OK if the vacancy is in sales or operations, or a functional area with direct bottom-line responsibility. But what about support functions?

No problem. Imagine you're interviewing a candidate for an HR job. Here's how it could possibly go:

Q. 'What one skill do you possess that will most impact our bottom line?'

A. 'I'm extremely good at ensuring compliance with regulations.'

It's not a terrible answer, because legal issues certainly do affect the bottom line. But where HR roles are concerned, ensuring compliance with legal (and ethical) guidelines should be a given. Saying you'll comply is like saying you'll come to work every day.

And maybe that's OK; maybe avoiding legal issues is all you care about. But I doubt it, because every support function should have a bottom-line impact. Every support function can directly affect costs and productivity, or even sales. So every employee in a support function should influence the bottom line. So the candidate might instead say, 'I'm extremely good at working with department heads to determine the unique skills and talents they need so I can find not just qualified candidates but exceptional candidates.'

Now we must like the sound of that. And you like the fact that they think about their job not just as a series of boxes to check, but one that has a broad impact on your business.

But then again, they could just be offering a platitude. What does that mean in practice? Try asking for an example - a natural question.

'A department manager gave me a list of qualifications for a sales manager position,' they might say. 'He said the right candidate needed a degree and at least ten years' experience in managing projects. I asked what he needed the person to actually do, and he said he needed someone to develop and release successful products. What he really needed was someone who had actually brought a number of products to market. Where that person went to school or whether they had been working in the field for 10 years was irrelevant.'

You like the sound of that, too. But there's a natural

question you can ask in response: 'Still, isn't it easier to give people what they ask for? Then it's their problem if the person selected doesn't work out, not yours.'

Maybe they have the right answer. Maybe they'll say it's everyone's problem if you don't find the perfect candidate.

And maybe you'll say, 'But what happens when a department manager feels you're trying to give him what you want instead of what he needs? Has that ever happened to you?'

And the conversation continues.

Try it. First, think about what you truly need: hard skills, soft skills, leadership skills. Don't think about the perfect candidate's qualifications but what the perfect person in the job will actually need to do. Then think of one question that can form the basis for a thoughtful conversation. You can use mine. Or you can use one of yours.

If you need a salesperson, your one question might be: 'If you could only choose one skill you possess, which will be most responsible for helping you land major customers for us?'

If you need an operations manager, your one question might be: 'What do you consider to be the toughest production challenge you've faced?'

If you need a programmer, your one question might be: 'What single project or task would you consider your most significant accomplishment in your career to date?'

Ask one question that will serve as the trunk of a huge tree, allowing you to branch off in a number of different directions. Then put away your papers and have a conversation. You'll learn a lot more than you would by following a canned interview guide, because the most revealing answers are to follow-up questions. Just listen. Then ask why. Or when. Or how a situation turned out. Or who actually did what. Or what made a success difficult to achieve, or what was learned from a failure.

You'll also enjoy the process more, because it will feel a lot more natural. Great candidates will also enjoy the process, because they will be able to relax and get into a conversational flow, and as a result give you their best. And isn't that what you really want from an interview?

19

RECRUITMENT – THE RED FLAGS

This level of focus on the recruitment process is because hiring the right people is now so important. While focusing on recruitment you must ensure that it is right first time. There are certain things to look out for - certain red flags - to ensure the process you go through does not result in recruiting the wrong people to fit the culture of your business.

So here are some points that you never, ever, wish to see on a CV:

1. Too many jobs. This is never a good sign - moving from one position to another can be a real downside to an employee. There need to be clear reasons why someone moves, because let's be honest, if you are successful and have added value to a business you would not want to leave, and the business would work hard to keep you. So what went wrong? Were they dismissed?

2.   Lying. it seems commonplace for lies and misleading information to creep onto CVs. But the truth will always come out. During the screening process it's important to invest time in questioning items you are unsure about. This will help unearth the truth about the individual. If you feel some of the information is untrue, I would counsel against recruiting.

3.   Lack of proficiency in MS Office. This is now becoming a prerequisite on CVs. It is no longer a skill but a necessity, so if someone presents it as a skill I would suggest they have little else to offer.

4.   Doers and non-doers. CVs are written in many ways, but be sure to dig into those parts where the individual talks about projects and work they have undertaken. The word 'strategy' is used regularly in a modern-day CV, and it can sometimes skirt around the situation. Actually doing a project and just being there when it takes place are two very different things, and taking credit for others' work is easy.

5.   'I'm an expert.' An over-used term. If someone truly is an expert they would not be looking for a job – people should be looking for them.

6.   Email address. During research amongst my peers in the industry I found these can be revealing. From the perspective of a small business looking for dynamic people to recruit, a standard Hotmail or AOL email address which has little or no resemblance to your name shows a lack of knowledge of the market and a limited ability – a more updated platform such as your own email address (you@yourname.com or yourname@gmail.com) shows an effort to stand out and be professional.

7. Many short-term appointments. Some candidates may have a lot of short-term posts or contract-based work on their CV. This might be a sign of a lack of commitment to a role or company, again offering doubts over the long-term development as an employee.

8. Output vs input. Many CVs are written with a focus on what tasks were carried out while in a role, but this suggests a failure to achieve. The focus in a CV should be on results achieved and targets hit. Focusing on the input suggests a lack of output. It is human nature for us to promote our successes, so if there is little about successes on the CV the candidate must have little to talk about.

9. Too many pages. The typical CV should really span no more than one page. It should be concise and to the point and manipulated for each role, targeting the points the company is looking for. Failure to make the CV concise suggests that being concise in the role will be difficult. There is an argument that it is difficult to be so concise, and that more pages are required. This is OK as long as the CN does not try to tell the company anything and everything about the span of a career. It's highly unlikely that work or training done 10 years ago will have any relevance to the marketplace today. Sadly the fast pace of the market has meant that people are constantly developing, and most of their development will come within the new role, just to keep up.

10. Poor spelling. The final point, but a key one, is around presentation and spelling. We all use a computer to write a CV, so checking for spelling and grammatical errors is paramount. If someone fails at this point it suggests a lack of attention to detail at work – a reason for instant rejection.

20

INTERVIEW QUESTIONS

Don't over-script your interview. You should be prepared to feed off the answers and simply talk to your candidate. A checklist of 100 questions can be worse than none at all and might lead to a nervous exchange of pre-prepared answers to questions they've run into time and again. Follow-up questions will help you go deeper and reveal far more about the candidate, including any chinks in their perfectly-prepared interview armour. Make sure you know how to spot a liar in your interviews too.

So feel free to chat and make the candidate feel comfortable and at ease. After all, you need to see whether they're culturally right for your business. But make sure you weave these essential questions into the interview. They'll reveal a lot about the individual and ensure you get the right person for the job.

1. *What happened the last time you made a major mistake, and how did you deal with it?*

2. *Can you give me example of when you exceeded expectations?*

3. *Why do you want to work for our company?*

4. *Where do you see yourself in five years?*

5. *Tell me about the last time you had to hit a tight deadline.*

6. *Do you have any questions?*

Summary

Interviewing someone isn't an exact science – it would be a lot easier if it were. The list above isn't an exhaustive list of questions to ask, and I'm sure if you searched on Google you'd find a lot more advice. At the end of the day you need insight and clear information that can make your hiring decision an easy one to make. Hopefully these questions will help you get one step closer to making that happen.

Conversely there is the other side of the recruitment journey - the recruiter, you or your managers. There are pitfalls you must learn to avoid, not just what you are looking for in potential new recruits; making it right from your end only enhances the prospect of a good intake. So some points to consider.

i. Establish clear expectation. You should never assume (my motto is actually 'assumptions are the mother of all f@*k ups') that the new employee, whether experienced or not, knows exactly what do to do and what your business is about. Expectations must be clearly defined by the business at the point of introduction. Knowing where both parties stand from the start facilitates a much more fluid line to a successful working relationship. I have always believed in a working statement or 'on-boarding statement' to help define expectations. This could be over a period of 90 days, six months etc, but it must state what will be achieved in this time and who is to measure it.

ii. Training delays. This is a real bugbear of mine personally and occurs all too often. When new recruits begin it's important that if there are training requirements, they are not delayed or put on hold. The training programme must be ready to go when the new employee enters the business; they need to feel the value being put into them from the day they begin. If training is left it will just never happen, leaving the new recruit to approach their new company from their own perspective. This will create a real danger that they will never grasp the company culture you have worked so hard to build.

iii. An eye on the future. Once the employee is up to speed it is important that development for the future is the next focus, with plans in place to actively grow the role they are performing. This is discussed in more detail in the following chapters.

21

RETENTION IS KEY

Much of the focus of this book is ultimately on employee retention, but this obviously applies only to the right people - those who have shown the right attitude and want to work alongside your company's vision. Although vision is not everything, employees still need to feel wanted. Have you heard the saying 'Employees don't leave companies, they leave managers'?

Today more people are leaving their jobs than ever. So are managers doing a bad job, or is the employee really leaving to move onwards and upwards? Failing to address bad management will leave any business at an increased risk of losing talented staff. Addressing the relationship between manager and employee is key, particularly when, in large part, the manager is the immediate day-to-day 'face' of your business.

However, let's not forget that there are occasions when staff turnover can actually benefit your business. You may feel fortunate when poor performers leave, and your business can get a welcome injection of fresh blood. There can also be a positive impact on the morale of the remaining team – particularly if the leaver had been lazy or disruptive.

The flip side of all this is the risk of losing valued and productive staff. As a business owner you need to try and think of work as fun and flexible. This can be applied to any size and type of business, creating more productive work environments at every level. Yet it can be daunting, because of the need to have a different outlook on the business now.

Most employees don't get out of bed each morning trying to hit a profit number. In most companies there are only a handful of people who truly care about the firm, or even understand exactly what it means to hit that number. As a manager, don't confuse your financial objectives with vision. Vision feeds financials, not the other way around. As a leader you need to drive the employees' enthusiasm.

When an employee leaves, always conduct an exit interview. This can not only produce qualitative data but give you a real feel for why people are moving on. Use this information to come up with action points moving forward for your business - learn from it and evolve, because the information gained is invaluable.

Always try and be flexible. Staff surveys regularly highlight the fact that flexible working patterns, shifts and home working really do enhance people's work/life balance. You'd be surprised at how many businesses still maintain a rigid working pattern – fixed start times, lunch hour etc. Recognising that many people have additional interests and responsibilities outside of work can really make a difference, and employees will see the business as an attractive place to work. You could trial a more flexible approach and see what the results show. This could be offered to a small group to begin with before filtering down to all levels.

Try and provide as much job security as possible. Key to this is communication. People naturally fear the worst, and these are financially trying times for businesses and individuals alike. Keep your employees in the loop, as security and stability are greatly valued by most people. Simple tips in communication are sometimes the most important aspects.

Creating career paths that are well communicated and understood by employees is not something most companies do well. Even in the best-case scenario where managers are holding regular performance reviews with their employees, these employees often don't understand how to move, either horizontally or vertically, within an organisation. Of course, not every employee is going to end up as the CEO. Likewise, a person who is brilliant at product design won't necessarily succeed in sales. But where an employee is worth retaining, a manager must make clear to them how and where they can expect to move forward on their career path. Many retention issues will be related to a member of staff who feels a lack of growth within their role or the scope of the role they undertake, which has in effect not been guided by the structure of the business. Giving guidelines and milestones to achieve the next levels within the structure will help to get to that point. Remember, your employees are your most valuable asset – if you look after them, they will make your business a success.

A phrase I have always believed helps encapsulate this feeling was said by the late, great Steve Jobs of Apple Inc: 'The only way to do great work is to love the work you do'. The business is responsible for creating the environment that offers this. Those who love what they do don't have to work a day in their lives. People who are able to bring passion to their business have a remarkable advantage, as that passion is contagious to customers and colleagues alike. Finding and increasing your passion will greatly affect your bottom line. Here is the reward for the introduction of these extra tiers of handwork.

22

THE YOUTH OF TODAY: APPRENTICESHIPS

What goes around comes around, they say, and as with fashion, it seems that business initiatives are always coming back around. In the days when I started in business the YTS and apprenticeships were all the rage, but in time and with improvements to funding opportunities to attend higher education these forms of access to the workplace dwindled. Now as costs for further education increase and university-educated individuals saturate the job market, apprenticeships and the push for young entrepreneurs are increasing.

Entering 2016 we saw the beginning of a fresh focus on apprenticeships, with a lot of funding available to businesses to take on young, hungry, mouldable people who can grow with a business. As discussed in previous chapters, what can be better than having people in your business ingrained with your ethos? This is surely a match made in heaven, although it has to be planned and delivered appropriately for it to blossom effectively and offer a real solution to long-term business recruitment.

Some points to consider when dealing with an apprentice:

i.   First identify the need for an apprentice (they may be your entire recruitment strategy) and get agreement from those in your business. Ensure you get the buy-in of those within the business, and engage with existing members of the business on the subject to generate positive interest.

ii. Do your research. As with any new initiative you will need to select an independent provider, and as with previous training initiatives there will be many providers out there looking to cash in on the money available to them, so get recommendations and shop around for a solid training provider. There are many organisations, such as Ofsted, where you can gain information and ensure you have a strong service level agreement.

iii. Once selected, you will need to agree a budget and available funding. As an employer it is your responsibility to contribute the wage for the apprentice, but this will be way below your current recruiting level and there is no recruitment fee, which lowers the risk in taking on the employee from the offset - win-win.

iv. Begin the recruitment process, using your provider as the conduit to allow access to candidates who have met agreed criteria specific to your organisation.

v.   The final step is to enter into a contract with the

successful candidate, but this needs a clear development path with full induction to the role. The rewards will come from getting it right from the outset. The people recruited through this method will welcome the opportunity, although it's the business's responsibility to make sure they are trained well; you have to remember these are inexperienced people presenting a blank canvas which can be crafted however you want. So make it count. Leaving them to their own devices will ultimately end in the parting of ways and a waste of time for everyone. It's a really good option for start-ups and evolving businesses which have a dynamic approach, not only cost effectively but also by having blank canvases which can be moulded by your businesses way of thinking from the offset. A key part for a start up by making the most of what resource is available to you at the time.

Apprenticeships have traditionally been viewed as the route for school-leavers wanting to learn a manual trade. This is no longer the case. Many industries now recognise that the applied learning and immersion offered by apprenticeship schemes can be of enormous benefit to both the organisation and the apprentice. For these reasons, apprenticeships are fast becoming an important tool for feeding the employment pipeline for many industries. They also satisfy the model of low-risk recruiting, helping to support methods already discussed throughout this book. This is essentially enabling employers to mould and create first-class service for years to come, with individuals groomed by an internal culture with common values.

Through providing formalised training, an

apprenticeship can help those working in many sectors to gain qualifications as they work. They are not just available for new recruits in an organisation; any employee can join an apprenticeship programme whilst either training towards their qualifications or looking for additional training. This is a great little loophole for helping with engagement through the development of your workforce. Not only will it work as a stepladder to securing advanced level training, it can enable organisations to adequately nurture employees to ensure top-quality service in their respective fields. I have personal experience of this process within the care sector, a notoriously low-paid sector where it is difficult to recruit. Offering different schemes to help grow staff motivation has been seen as welcome added value to the job. In turn it has created a higher quality of workforce, who wish to grow internally or maybe it helps them with the next step in their careers. Richard Branson has said: 'Train people well enough so they can leave; treat them well enough so they don't want to'. This is always worth remembering when approaching this type of process, but essentially it is more of a risk not to do it than it is to ignore it.

In my own experience of offering apprenticeships as part of the overall learning and development programme, I have seen employee engagement, and as a direct correlation staff retention rates, increase. This has a positive knock-on effect for your clients or service users, as they will speak to the same people and work in partnership with the same faces and voices, building customer retention for your brands.

Apprenticeships can lay the foundations for training, set a clear progression timeline and encourage continuous education, but they are not a one-size-fits-all tool. They should be considered and developed closely with the management teams who will be running them on a daily basis to ensure the requirements are met to enable the individual, and indeed the organisation, to thrive because of it. As long as they are approached in the right way, these can help get the right people into your industry, people who can grow with your organisation.

In most cases with apprenticeships you will need to link in with a strong training provider partner. These companies have the right access to market funding, which takes away much of the headache, although as with any money-making opportunity sadly there will be those looking for the commission element who will fail to deliver for your business. So doing the research and getting advice from your locality will help you to get it right first time. This is something I didn't do the first time I got involved with training, and my gung ho approach led to me getting my fingers burnt, so learn from my mistakes. It's all about a shared philosophy, but I'm sure this is something you do with all new suppliers to your business.

Overall, introducing apprenticeships into your organisation is a great opportunity to pave the way for hungry individuals to get into your industry, whatever it may be. Try it out - run a pilot during your next recruitment drive, and try a measured approach for recruiting two people into similar roles, one through normal recruiting methods and the second via an apprenticeship route. You can then measure the value output cost of recruiting, cost of training and then the final product 6-12 months down the line. This could be a valuable step-change for further recruitment development.

23

THE ROLE OF MENTORING

From my early twenties I was always heavily involved in my own development and was offered many platforms to progress above my academic-only status, as it was. In corporate life mentoring programmes are pretty much industry standard and to some extent natural for graduate to professional roles. The thought that you wouldn't have a mentor would almost be frowned upon, but in truth those of us who went through such a programme rarely saw any real benefits at that stage in our careers.

Why? Is it because mentoring was seen as a standardised process allocated to individuals based on the job they are in? Again this is a mistake - mentoring is about development, being defined as 'the practice of assuaging a junior member of staff to the care of a more experienced person who assists him or her in their career'.

How can you mentor without defining or developing the

plan for someone's career path within the business? This is key to determining what mentoring is required. More often than not this service will come from external organisations who are dedicated to offering impartial but focused mentoring for people on the journey to the next level. Every job should have the potential to lead to greater things. Exceptional bosses take the time to develop employees for the job they some day hope to land, even if that job is with another company.

How can you know what an employee hopes to do some day? Ask. Employees will only care about your business after you first show you care about them. One of the best ways is to show that while you certainly have hopes for your company's future, you also have hopes for your employees' futures.

You are probably thinking - this is more cost to the business. Why would we consider it? Because if employees are mentored on what they want to do then, it becomes a motivation through the control of their own destiny.

The long-term return on investment will come from the fact that the employee will remain loyal to the business because of the value they have seen from this investment. Remember, not all rewards are visible as monetary values. There are many great mentoring groups in the country; some are specific to individuals, while some are focused on teams and managers.

The beauty of focusing on mentoring is the understanding that everyone in the company at every level is constantly learning. Certain programmes I have been involved in have worked from CEO down to sales desk team members, which has enabled real fluidity in the management as it removes the next problem:

The glass wall

Just saying 'hello' can go a long way with your colleagues. As we discussed right at the beginning, there is still a feeling in some businesses that the leaders of the company are unapproachable. A glass office wall separates the senior manager from the operational workforce. Companies still embedding this culture are failing big time. Putting up a wall between leaders and teams brings about a sense of depersonalisation which tends to affect relationships, making people feel unable to trust the process. It is difficult to see how to manage your way out once you are operating like this. The mentoring process can begin to bring down barriers such as this when you are working across the business at all levels.

Bad, bad habits can begin to appear when you're offering a mentoring programme, and being quick to identify them can be powerful in staff development and avoid the risk of the programme failing.

1. Ask, don't tell.

When people are told they need to change a habit, the typical response is to rebel. Whether people change is largely determined by why they change. And they are most successful at changing when they choose to change. Mentoring is often imposed, rather than invited. Successful coaching assiduously avoids any approach that might provoke resistance to the attempt at change. The trick is to not lecture your employees about their bad habit, or tell them it is hurting their chances of promotion. Instead, ask questions and treat the coaching session like an interview.

Help people to uncover motivations they already have. Hopefully through the recruitment format these motivations would have already been understood, and the development programme is born out of these notions.

2. Enable people, don't motivate.

Once you are able to help people uncover their motivations to change, you need to enable them to change. Many coaches and leaders make the mistake of 'overvaluing motivation.' When an employee tends to procrastinate, we tend to think they are lazy. If an employee has a bad temper, we say they are overly aggressive. But these behaviours are not so simple. Attributing behaviour to dispositional factors is a mistake. Instead of just going after motivations, a great mentor will go after 'ability barriers.' One example: 'If someone struggles with procrastination, a good mentor might suggest tactics for better managing interruptions'. For your short-tempered employee, help him pinpoint emotional triggers. Find out what's getting in the way of your talented employees' ability to work well.

3. Explore the context of behaviours.

When a mentor focuses solely on the employee, not much change can take place. An employee's motives and abilities do not live in a vacuum. You need to address the four sources of influence: 'fans', 'accomplices', 'incentives' and 'environment.' Are other people, the office culture and the work environment contributing to the problem? These four factors can confound even the most resolute people in their efforts to change. But our study shows that when all of these sources of influence are engaged positively in the effort, the likelihood of rapid and sustainable change increases tenfold. If you find an executive is giving your short-tempered employee a pat on the back for yelling at a team member, you need to make sure it doesn't happen again. If bad behaviour is met with silence, you're contributing to the problem. And if bad employees are promoted, you're effectively incentivising people to be bad.

24

DEVELOPING AS ONE

Everyone likes to feel a part of something bigger. Everyone loves to feel that sense of teamwork and *esprit de corps* that turns a group of individuals into a real team. The best business missions involve making a real impact on the lives of the customers you serve. Let employees know what you want to achieve for your business, for your customers, and even your local community, if you can - let them create a few business missions of their own.

Feeling a true sense of purpose starts with knowing what to care about and, more importantly, why to care. This is within the core values of the company, developed in its early stages. Development can come in different forms based on individuals. Employees want to know they have a future in a company; let's be honest, no one wants to keep constantly searching for a job. As we have identified throughout, the main reasons for leaving are usually intangible feelings and personal feedback rather than financial reward. Therefore a focus on a career is crucial; this will help them to feel more at home with the company.

This comes with encouragement of learning, yet many businesses lack the access to availability to knowledge and self-development. I have always asked in interviews, especially for sales roles, what books the candidates were currently reading, what blogs they read and if they had seen any interesting TED talks/online video media. Why is this? Because I wanted to understand the thirst for self-development of an individual. These were not trick questions but helped ascertain how people perceive their own development. I personally as a business owner am constantly reading, or rather listening to, audio books on various business approaches, and on psychology, usually mixed in with the odd fictional title to help relieve the barrage of new ideas.

Simple encouragement for learning could be giving your staff access to a collection of motivational reading or setting up an internal website with access to online collateral or audio books, especially ones you have read as a leader and manager yourself. This not only encourages the ownership of personal development but helps people understand the direction you may be going in as a leader, and can offer support to your own directions. It can also be linked to your industry as a specific knowledge base, whether it be manufacturing or design; you can create a go-to knowledge base for your employees to help them to become more engrossed in your industry. This very much supports a bottom-up approach to development, breeding hungry culture-led employees working to the values of the business. Long term the attempts to break their habits and leave this type of environment gives you as a leader a more educated workforce who understand your business and therefore work in similar ways to you. This strategy will really enable strong development to get under way within your workforce.

A major outcome of development for people is recognition through internal promotion within an organisation, and there are conditions applying to this which people should be aware of.

Conditions for promotion

1. The job has to be big enough: We might have an incredible manager of something, but we don't need a director of it because the job isn't big enough. If the incredible manager left, we would replace them with a manager, not a director.

2. The person has to be a superstar in their current role. Could you get to the next level job in your current organisation if applying from outside and you knew their talents well? Could you get the next level job at a peer firm that knew their talents well?

3. These people provide an extraordinary role model of your cultures and values. The conditions should become prerequisites when looking at who and why a promotion path is created for your people. There has to be a reason, and an excellent reason at that, as to why people are in this position. Your culture must drive your employees to excel to achieve the next level, giving your business the most from them at a particular time to warrant an upturn in their career. You can't just promote for the sake of it.

Input should be bottom up

To encourage development and excel in order to achieve promotion, you need engaged employees who want to have ideas; take away opportunities for them to make suggestions, or instantly disregard their ideas without consideration, and they immediately disengage. That's why exceptional bosses make it really easy for employees to offer suggestions. They ask leading questions. They probe gently. They help employees to feel comfortable proposing new ways to get things done. When an idea isn't feasible, they always take the time to explain why. Great leaders know that employees who make suggestions care about the company, so they ensure those employees know their input is valued and appreciated.

This is an aspect of the bottom-up approach that many businesses need adhere to and ensure they are not becoming too top heavy. This mentality follows on from our earlier discussions on a flatter culture.

While studying for my degree at Nottingham Trent University Business School, I found that part of any honours degree was to prepare a dissertation. Having taken a sandwich course involving a year in industry which took up the entire third year of my degree, I decided to focus my dissertation around this year in industry, which was not a prerequisite. The focal point of this paper was 'user involvement', and it related to the association utilising the operational level workforce of users in the implementation of a multi-million-pound customer relationship management (CRM) system. I focused the paper on the lack of operational level input in its development, the failure being that the leaders of the company implanted a system which would fundamentally change the way people worked within their daily routine without ever taking consideration of those people who would actually use it.

The findings clearly showed some areas of concern:

i.   Poor uptake.

ii. Demotivated staff.

iii. Continued updating.

iv. Extensive training programmes.

The cost and the requirement of management time to save this project was extensive; this could have been removed if the end users had been involved from the start.

This issue is present in many management decisions whereby a good idea for the leaders may not actually be the most effective way forward for the business as a whole. There is a need sometimes for engaged employees who have ideas; take away opportunities for them to make suggestions, or instantly disregard their ideas without consideration, and they immediately disengage. This can have a long-term effect on the business as a whole. That's why exceptional bosses make it easy for employees to offer suggestions. It brings long-term loyalty with focused, energised employees.

25

KEEPING YOUR PEOPLE WANTING MORE

Sickness and absenteeism are a great loss to your effectiveness, whether from general absence or long-term illness. Real sickness cannot be helped and should not be over-scrutinised but managed accordingly, but increased unjustified absence means some of your people may not actually want to come to work. This may be hard to take, but it happens in every business and has to be accepted.

You should aim to reduce absenteeism, as it has a huge knock-on effect in terms of time, which eventually comes to a monetary value. This is not necessarily measurable, although it should be.

There are several ideas you can build on to help improve the absence problem:

i.   Build outdoor exercise into your team's weekly routine.

ii. Customise the workplace: add pieces of art to project creative visuals for a more exciting environment.

iii. Introduce more plants and greenery into the office.

iv. Liven up your meetings: include less text and more attention-grabbing, colourful imagery in presentation materials.

v.   Ditch email and focus on face-to-face communication and interaction with colleagues, especially those on site.

I worked within a company in the south east who took some of these ideas on board from an early stage of its growth. It has seen its workforce stay loyal and continually grow. It made simple additions to the above criteria, utilising very cost-effective ideas which created maximum reward for the employees.

Promoting wellness through building exercise into your weekly teams' routines will always create a happier, more productive workforce. Investing in keeping the workforce healthy will bring rewards long term through a positive staff feeling. Some examples of this include:

Low cost options

i.   Running/cycling club.
ii. Tabata clubs.
iii. Walking.
iv. Linked charity events (training as a group for a common fundraising goal).

Investment required

i.   In-office fitness sessions (PT).
ii. Subsidise gym membership.
iii. Sports/competitive teams (a five-a-side football team, for example).

Getting involved in charity events is a great way for people to give something back to the communities they work in and offers an added sense of achievement within the company, something people may not have felt they could do without the involvement of others. A key way to do this and engage with the communities you work in is to create an internal committee formed of employees who can donate their time and skills to good causes. This is a risk in terms of the time taken up, but a reward comes not only from ongoing employee engagement with your business values but increased promotion of your business in the communities that you are supporting.

The healthy business

This leads to a new extension for businesses which has become more focused, in the form of a healthy business. The Marmot Review and the features within the new Liverpool workplace charter have made real steps with regards to guidance in improving the workplace. Many people do not believe in this idea of a healthy business, as it felt to be too much effort and they adopt a 'why should I bother?' attitude. But the effects of the extra mile in terms of your workforce will always be beneficial.

The healthy business profile is a little like the common values discussed in the early chapters. I think businesses see them as something for larger corporate organisations and feel that their investment in time will not be reflected in the return. This is again a risk businesses take, but it can be achieved in small businesses, and step by step a roll-out of healthy business protocols can put the finishing touches to a transformation.

So what is this all about? It's about wellbeing, a buzz word of our times but actually one that's worth sitting up and paying attention to. The wellbeing of staff brings about some keys strengths for a business.

Wellbeing suggestions:

i.   Smoke-free days.

ii. Monthly wellbeing focuses (cancer, stress etc).

iii. Fruit Mondays - promotion of fruit in the office.

iv. Online health plans.

v.   Subsidised health plans.

vi. Goal creation based on environment and wellbeing.

vii. Subsidised gym membership.

The wellbeing initiative is a fundamental change, making employers more accountable for their employees in all of their activities rather than just their work-related responsibilities. The end goal is creating a functional workforce, working not just for the business but crucially, with the business.

Wellbeing initiatives can generally improve productivity, employee morale, business profile and internal competitiveness, thereby reducing absence from sickness, staff turnover and even accidents and injuries, which can become the bane of active jobs. Even if this is due to lack of sleep through a poor diet or standard of living, if this was in the construction industry the aftermath could be catastrophic. This helps the business to become proactive with its workforce in more ways than one. A reactive business is an ignorant business which will ultimately suffer poor profitability.

In recent years the focus on healthy businesses has become more prominent, with many government initiatives, yet despite a concerted effort from employers to invest in staff wellbeing, the British economy wastes £100 billion each year on ineffective and poorly-planned health initiatives. Dame Carol Black is a pioneer in this subject and I have attended many of her seminars over a 12-month period of research on the subject. A clear statement emerged: 'The return on the balance sheet from investing in workplace health is, over a five-year period, normally at least double and sometimes treble the amount spent'. This is a key aspect of establishing an improved workforce. It is clear once again that investment in initiatives can bring long-term productivity benefits for your organisations.

I do suggest that you make a point of sitting down in your next board meeting or management meeting and having a look at what you are doing about health. Are you achieving anything? Don't be afraid if the answer is no, because this is a good thing. You can look at a new blueprint for these initiatives and make initial low-cost attempts to build a health strategy which will keep employees interested. But never forget that like many things we are exploring, the best approaches are those designed with input from the staff groups themselves with the support of senior management. This increases engagement in any activity, enhancing its likelihood of a successful impact on the organisation in the long run.

26

THE ETHICAL BUSINESS

Ethics is a word that feels as if it can have different meanings depending on its context, but for our purposes it boils down to a practical question: what is your business giving back to the community in which it operates? Some see this as its corporate social responsibility, but it is more than this. It's not just being a healthy business that matters to employees. As I've said, motivating your people is different for everyone, so you need to cover as many bases as you can. Not always easy, but if you do it as part of your strategy then these areas will grow naturally.

Being compassionate has now become a competitive advantage, while focusing purely on profit is seen as a short-term fix, not a long-term vision. People within and outside the business you operate will be interested in how you behave ethically as an organisation, and make purchases based on this. Promoting your good behaviour can only increase the profile of the business to all stakeholders.

Sir Richard Branson speaks of this in his blogs and supports an ethical strategy. 'Almost everybody will choose the products or services of an ethically sound company over its less scrupulous competitors,' he says - and here is a man who really does know what he is talking about. Employees will want to work for and be motivated by the fact that a company is thinking ethically when it comes to the way it operates.

It's worth asking your employees what they think of the business in terms of its ethics. Ask them open questions, whether in a questionnaire, in a meeting or as an online survey (use www.surveymonkey.com, great for setting up free response-based surveys). This will help you and your teams explore the strategy for the future, and ticks another box in the process of involving your staff in the development of the strategy, which in turn helps to gain their buy-in to whatever you choose to do. This will begin to take shape with just some simple steps around engagement.

The digital workforce

As I have been involved in the telecommunications industry since I graduated from university and still operate a business in this sector, I think it would be wrong not to discuss this in some detail, without being too technical and going off topic, of course. More information on this is available from my company website.

A digital workplace reflects the concept that there is a virtual equivalent to the physical workplace, and that it needs to be planned and managed coherently because it is fundamental to people's productivity, engagement and working health. The notion of 'workplace' itself is ill defined, so the shape of a digital workplace will vary between organisations.

The digital workplace provides organisations with the following services or capabilities:

- Communication and employee engagement.
- Collaboration.
- Finding and sharing of information and knowledge.
- Business applications (process-specific and employee self service).
- Agile working – the ability to be productive any time and place.

There are major benefits for an organisation in operating a digital workplace. This approach is ever more required in the dynamic world of SME businesses with the increased demand for ad hoc meetings. On-the-spot collaboration helps to save time and money and increase efficiency – effective collaboration tools available to businesses are facilitating this demand for fast and now.

The fundamentals of controlling costs, retaining customers and gaining competitive advantage are still universally seen as the three business requisites driving most organisations. Underlying these goals is the need for firms to develop and bring to market new products/services ever more quickly and provide customer service excellence to new and existing clients.

Traditionally many organisations have worked in what many authors term 'silos', a mindset more present within large corporate departments or specific sectors who wish not to share information with others in the same company. We have sadly all experienced this in some way or another.

Such silos waste resources, kill productivity and jeopardise the achievement of set goals. Modern management thinking should be that leaders should tear down silos by moving past behavioural issues and addressing the contextual problems that are present at the heart of the organisation, so as to provide a unified vision of the business.

Until recent times however, the communication tools available to businesses to support this breakout from the silo effect using unified communications (UC) have themselves been cumbersome, inflexible, difficult to implement and use, and above all, very costly to purchase. In this creative digital age, following the widespread introduction of cloud-based communications, this no longer applies. Here, applications that were traditionally located in servers based in the business's head offices are instead supplied to users via networks connected to servers in remote data centres.

Users for the cloud-based communications model benefit from this in a number of ways:

1. The applications are provided as an operational expense (OPEX) and generally on a per user, per product basis, as opposed to a large up-front capital expenditure (CAPEX) project plus on-going maintenance/service charges throughout the duration of the contract. This helps businesses of all sizes to utilise the benefits of these services.

2. Network connectivity can often be bundled in with the cloud OPEX costs instead of becoming an additional line item on every bill. This is important, as the use of faster internet connectivity is required and this is reflected in higher costs, so it is always useful to link the products and services together.

3. User flexibility is enhanced through only being charged for the services you use rather than the total capability of the system. For example, if you purchased a 50-seat call centre application, once you have paid for the on-site traditional installation a service charge appropriate to a 50-user system would be levied monthly or yearly for the remainder of the contract period – say 5 or 7 years typically. If the user downscaled the call centre to say 30 agents in year 2 of the contract the CAPEX on the premises solution would remain at the 50 seats originally purchased. In a cloud-based solution the cost would simply reduce on a monthly basis to the new number of 30 seats. Equally cloud-based solutions can be scaled up to say 60 or 70 seats for seasonal periods or high retail points (such as Christmas) that occur within your business model. This rules out any other CAPEX costs which could hamper long-term profitability.

4. Typically users of a CAPEX or traditional model of communications are faced with software upgrade costs on a regular basis. These can be substantial if you want to keep the solution current. With a cloud-based system these tend to be FREE and part and parcel of the overall service wrap and deployment.

Whilst these can be viewed as generic benefits of using cloud-based communications, it is equally important to examine how using 'software as a service' (SaaS) can provide increases in productivity to an organisation by improving the opportunities for greater collaboration between the workforces and greater access to each other as people. This already happens in our private lives through the use of social media, so utilising similar platforms in the business life can be truly effective.

Let's look at the typical applications in SaaS solutions that can bring an organisation together. Stand-alone applications or pieces of software purchased by businesses over the years are the equivalent of working in silos, sadly, with multiple accesses and user screens further confusing staff and increasing training costs. Just as company silos need to come together and work for the improvement of the business as a whole, so do computing and communication applications. This can come with research into effective SaaS integrations in your business environment.

Through a single-user interface, applications that should be considered central to business operations would include voice telephony, internet-based trunking, voicemail and collaboration applications such as chat messaging, customer relationship management software, presence information, desk-to-desk video and audio conferencing, without being too exhaustive.

The latest in SaaS solutions are using the internet web browsers for voice and video call set up, which means no specific additional user equipment is required. Take Skype from Microsoft and FaceTime from Apple as easy examples – just requiring access to the web. As well as reducing costs considerably this helps with mobile working, adding to the ability of your business to become more dynamic and employee-focused. Many can easily access these features not only from a laptop but from their own smartphone or tablet, anywhere in world.

Unified communications or Software as a Service improve productivity and save organisations valuable time and money. According to market research undertaken by Chadwick Martin Bailey:

■ 49% of user organisations save up to 20 minutes per employee daily by reaching workers on the first try.

- 46% of user organisations realise travel savings of more than five days per employee annually.

- 68% of user organisations report productivity improvements between geographically-dispersed functional groups.

- 50% of user organisations save up to 20 minutes per employee daily from more efficient message management.

- Over 75% of user organisations experience an improved productivity of employees across locations due to voice and video conferencing.

- 67% of user organisations report increased mobile worker productivity and faster problem solving.

All the above points not only benefit the business itself but directly affect the happiness and motivation of the workforce, offering flexibility and more often than not improved retention numbers. Remember, not everything is about money; facilitating flexibility for many is now a prerequisite of a working lifestyle balance.

With this collaboration effect, management today need to have a unified vision for their organisation, which in turn necessitates ensuring all users are willing to adopt the SaaS tools in order to enable collaborations.

Getting maximum productivity out of a knowledge workforce regardless of where they are is critical to maintaining any competitive advantage. Businesses therefore need their critical workforces to perform smarter, faster and more productively. Achieving that goal requires embedding collaborative technologies deep into process and incentivising collaborative behaviours. This is transforming the way businesses turn knowledge into action.

Collaboration platforms should do more than help employees to talk about their work; they should create new ways for employees to do their work, increasing the enjoyment and focus they bring to the job. What an amazing win-win thought process that is!

Meetings in the office can be great when everyone is based there, but over the years I have seen the loss in motivation that results from widely-dispersed workforces and a demand for long commutes to attend meetings. This is one of the most counterproductive elements and can harm retention numbers dramatically. The digital workforce opportunity offers the chance for businesses to change this mindset forever, enabling all employees to be engaged in decision making wherever they may be in the world.

Following on from this, I admit that there is a lot of jargon and use of industry acronyms, which can really deter people from caring about this stuff and recognising its importance. Even if this is not you, I implore you to delegate a member of your team to investigate the communications infrastructure within your business. When done properly, it can have a dramatic effect on business processes and cost efficiencies. When I personally support businesses over this function, 95% of the time we are able to find areas where the business is simple wasting money on services they do not use, and not utilising the availability of digital effectiveness. So take some time and make sure you have a scalable communications plan for your business.

27

THE IMPORTANCE OF A BUSINESS COMMUNICATIONS PLAN

Now I'm sure your company has a business plan and a commercial strategy. Chances are it also has an annual sales and marketing plan, projections and targets to support. But does it have a technology or communications plan? According to research, more than 50% of businesses don't have one, even though the majority of businesses now have a very heavy reliance on technology.

In the past, bandwidth was extremely expensive and phone calls to international customers or keeping in touch with a mobile workforce cost a small fortune. It was simply not available for SME businesses focusing on revenue growth, due to the large CAPEX requirements. For a small business, implementing a cost-effective disaster recovery plan or communications network was nigh on impossible. Now, however, with the constantly-evolving world of telecommunications and IT, cutting edge solutions are not only cost effective but easy to implement, and they provide a whole world of opportunity to their adopters.

So if you don't have a technology plan already, now might be the time to think about creating one. The technology choices you make as a business will have significant financial and compatibility consequences for the future.

Of course, there is no one-size-fits-all type exercise. Your strategy will be unique to the needs of your business. However, it should take into account some of the following.

How do you use technology now, and how will you use it in the future?

Almost every aspect of business is now affected by technology in some way, whether it be accounting systems, HR systems or traditional telephony. How do these systems work at the moment and are they allowing you to stay competitive? Take the time to look at this now.

Do you have the right solutions in place? If not, why?

Once you have established how you use technology now and how you would like to in the future, you need to ensure you have the right connectivity and software and systems to meet your needs now and moving forward. Function, compatibility with legacy systems, cost, ease of use/implementation and scalability are all important issues to consider.

Are you allowing for advances in technology?

Your communications plan, like your business plan, should be a working document. Technology is constantly evolving and you need to ensure that you allow for elements of change. One of the key things businesses need to allow for is the growth in requirement for bandwidth for your business. Nielsen's law of internet bandwidth states that high-end users' requirement will grow by 50% a year. Based on that, if you need a 10mb connection now, then you will need a 75mb connection in five years' time. Make the allowances now, to save time-consuming and costly infrastructure changes in the future.

If you lost all your telecommunications services tomorrow,
how would it affect your business?

This is a very important question that all business owners or IT managers should be asking. If we were to lose all IT and telecommunications systems tomorrow for an hour, or a day, or a week, how would it affect the business? For many businesses, a day without telephones, email or internet could cost them anything from a couple of thousand pounds to a couple of hundred thousand. For some, a catastrophic loss of data could spell the end for the business. (A recent study from Gartner Inc. found that 90 percent of companies that experience data loss go out of business within two years.)

Implementing a suitable business continuity strategy can seem expensive and is often overlooked. When things are going well, people are happy to take the risk, thinking that it will never happen to them, but when it comes to business-critical systems and the future of your business, prevention is definitely better than cure.

28

TALKING ABOUT COMMUNICATION

Why have we left it until now to look at communications? Because communication between employers and employees is almost the final string to the bow, as many of the initial tasks become a working reality. If you were to ask any employee about a key challenge within their current work environment, most often communication issues will top the list, or maybe second behind benefits. There is so much available on the subject out in the ether, but sadly, not all good practice seems to be adhered to. So why do businesses still face issues when it comes to communication?

Many believe it's because communication is always reviewed from the communicator's/business owner's point of view rather than that the listener/employee. Any communicator must understand the needs and perspectives of those they wish to communicate with. So the information being shared must be of interest, useful and/or simply relevant to their daily activity. We go to that word 'engagement' again - is the communication engaging employees to listen and process effectively, or sadly are they just switching off?

Some points for communication can include these following four steps, heavily discussed in Dale Carnegie's training on leadership and management.

i.   Entertain - Make the message interesting to listen to, be humorous or include interesting facts related to the subject matter. I personally have always found video a great way to engage during communication, especially in large groups. With multiple clips on any subject matter available on YouTube, it is always a good engagement tool to link a pithy video into your communications. During sales briefings on getting the most out your day, I would always refer to a clip from the Will Smith film *The Pursuit of Happyness*. The film has a great moment about selling and how to achieve more in less time. It worked overtime to get people on board to the next part of the communication.

ii.   Inform - Once people are engaged, make sure your material is informative. The last thing you need is meetings for meetings sake. This gets you and your teams nowhere and essentially wastes time.

iii. Convince - Make sure that the people you are engaging will listen and take on board the specifics of your communication. Compel people to act on the communication, or indeed encourage the additional input with the current meeting. Remember discussion is good.

iv. Communicate to action - This is the next step, the energy behind the communication. Always having an outcome in mind before communicating is essential to allow some measurement of whether the communication was successful and whether it needs changing for the next attempt. For individuals to achieve, a goal must be communicated.

More often than not, an action or measurement is not identified by the communication. The result is disappointment for the communicator/presenter, because the goal they wanted is not achieved. Furthermore there will be frustration from the employees, as they are confused by the communication's failure to demonstrate a benefit to them or their work environment. The next steps must be clear and concise, and well planned in advance of the communication. This preparation will bring more valuable outcomes for all concerned.

There are still risks with communication, including a desire to avoid telling, or what I call 'one-way contact'. I was brought up with this, and I have been making the point throughout this book that you can't order people around and expect the best results. You always have to be concerned about who is listening to the message and what their perspectives are. Some may think this is a lot to put into a message, but you have to look at the risks of not doing it properly. Poor delivery of communication will only lead to one definite outcome - a frustrated workforce. So like it or not you have to engage with employees on their level, getting them to buy into whatever you are selling.

So communication is critical for a business's success. As business leaders we can all continually improve the focus and purpose of communications. Always explain why your message is important with clear, concise points which show benefits to those who are listening in a way which achieves an outcome.

In your next meeting, follow a couple of simple new steps and see how you get on this time with what return you gain. First, actually plan the discussion, pinpoint your outcomes and engage the listeners with them. Second, find some interesting content, whether it be video or event quotations from well-known outlets (these are easy to find on the internet), and finally engage in discussions on the goals for the listeners, allowing them to buy in to the message at hand. This will work for every meeting, 1-2-1 or presentation.

29

CONCISE OBJECTIVES

Most people don't mind a boss who is strict, demanding, and quick to offer (not always positive) feedback, as long as he or she treats every employee fairly. (Great bosses treat every employee differently, but they also treat every employee fairly. There's a big difference.) Exceptional bosses know that the key to showing employees they are consistent and fair is communication: the more employees understand why a decision was made, the less likely they are to assume unfair treatment or favouritism.

While every job should offer some degree of independence, every job does also need basic expectations for how specific situations should be handled. Criticise an employee for offering a discount to an irate customer today even though yesterday that was standard practice and you make that employee's job impossible. Few things are more stressful than not knowing what is expected from one day to the next.

Are your objectives meaningful?

When an exceptional boss changes a standard or guideline, he or she communicates those changes first - and when that is not possible, they take the time to explain why they made the decision, and what's expected in the future.

Almost everyone is competitive, and often the best employees are extremely competitive - especially with themselves. Meaningful targets can create a sense of purpose and add a little meaning to even the most repetitive tasks.

Plus, goals are fun. Without a meaningful goal to shoot for, work is just work, and let's be honest, no one likes work.

Realise that *change does not happen unless you are in it.* As a leader of your team, organisation or business, many times we are very good at initiating 'change' but not very good at putting ourselves inside the very change that we are expecting to be made by those around us.

How many times during a meeting or when approaching a time-sensitive deadline for a project have you experienced a hard time getting everything needed out of your team? You had a meeting to discuss the deliverables needed and assign tasks with deadlines, yet it seems that you spent so much time having to restate and overstate what you need to have produced, only to find that what is actually delivered is not what you were hoping for. There are two reasons for this type of outcome – lack of a sense of urgency and poor communication. When you have a culture where everything is 'urgent' and needed right now, it's hard for your team to distinguish what is really urgent from what's just noise.

Ultimately everyone becomes numb to the request. The way to combat this is through better communication to your team about the deliverables you need to have completed.

When it comes to urgency and how to best communicate it, inserting YOU in the deliverables shows your teams that you are just as accountable as they are for the overall completion of the task. Constant urgency communicates poor planning and a lack of focus that make it hard for people to follow. Remember, everyone loves order and sound direction, no matter how time sensitive the deliverable is.

Normally when we need something quickly, we name-drop the person who asked for it. It's an assumption that if the manager or their manager asked for it, it means a 911 phone call to the team members. If leaders knew how people communicated the task and deliverables down the line, it might shock them. A better way to communicate is to give your team the WHY. 'Why' is such a simple question, but such a powerful one. If you lead with the why of what is needed, you are solving the understanding equation: (why + what = understanding).

Here are two quick things you can do in order to ensure the next task or deliverables are done with accuracy:

1. Instead of relying on the URGENT subject line of an email, meet in person with your top influencer of the team and discuss what is needed and provide options. Share with them the objective, timeline and important task. Then ask 'How can we best go about this?' This allows for input from the team, against just telling everyone what to do.

2. Pick one of the tasks and say YOU will complete it. Team members will feel more responsibility when you are involved in the overall deliverables. The benefit to this

approach is that you get to experience the process with them. Most leaders today feel they are entitled to delegate because of their position and never get dirty, but every now and then being involved helps the morale of the team.

Two more Cs

Consequence and consistency, in my opinion, are the two most important steps in delivering anything with intent in life, let alone business. When people talk to me about their businesses and seek advice I have the usual patter of commentary on business development and goal setting etc. But in truth, by following the 2 Cs in everything you do you can't go far wrong. When guiding employees it can feel like gathering the herd, overseeing an extended family; I was once told that staff are like children and need constant contact.

Another analogy is that managing staff is like captaining a narrowboat. You can go up river or down river but you can't go sideways, so set barriers.

Both these thoughts still for me lead back to the 2 Cs - be consistent and ensure there is a consequence. Once this is clear many managerial situations become easy to process. For example, having a consistent process to managing performance, whether good or bad, leaves little room for demotivation. If people do X the response will be Y - by have clear indications of what these two benchmarks are time after time, the habit will be set that this is the expectation and this is how they should behave. Conversely, having clear consequences for actions again enables a clear understanding of what happens. If someone has achieved X they will receive Y, and vice versa, if they have failed to achieve X they will not receive Y.

BY stepping away and looking at the internal processes of an organisation you can begin to determine whether you have these types of guidelines. Take it away as an exercise and ask the following questions:

i.   Are we consistent in our HR message?

ii. Are we clear on the consequence of success or failure?

iii. Do we have a process in place for the following situation, should it arise? In many cases there may be no process.

The list could be exhaustive, but just thinking about a few ways to improve in these areas will have a massive impact on the habits of employees. If everyone know what happens when they do a particular thing, the business can almost manage itself. The consistent message through this book has been - put in the hard work at the beginning, so that in the long run as more people come on board, the tone for the organisation is set.

It will always need maintenance and a constant eye to ensure it matches the ever-changing needs of a business, but the same rules will always apply - are we being consistent, and is there a consequence for the actions of our people (good or bad)?

We are creatures of habit. We gather in groups, we all look for a leader, we all dream, and all men sadly fail to return the toilet seat to its rightful place. The same applies in the workplace. If we want people to work in a certain way, it must be ingrained in the philosophy of the organisation for which they work. Many of the issues touched on in this book relate to systems and processes, which will ultimately, if operated effectively, create habits in our workforce – they will become the culture. Protecting these habits by influencing positive habits within your workforce will help to develop sustainable, motivated employees who give 100% to your vision as a leader.

30

AUTONOMY AND INDEPENDENCE

Great businesses are built on optimising processes and procedures. Still, every task doesn't deserve a best practice or a micro-managed approach. (I'm looking at you, manufacturing.)

Engagement and satisfaction are largely based on autonomy and independence. I care when it's 'mine.' I care when I'm in charge and feel empowered to do what's right. Plus, freedom breeds innovation: even heavily process-oriented positions have room for different approaches. (Still looking at you, manufacturing.)

Whenever possible, give your employees the autonomy and independence to work the way they work best. When you do, they almost always find ways to do their jobs better than you imagined possible.

Creating a high-trust culture

When people think of their most rewarding professional achievements, what usually come to mind is their genuine accomplishments - the times when they faced challenges, beat the odds, or created something that stood the test of time.

Though our most meaningful work is often the result of intensive effort and focus, most of the time we don't do it alone. Colleagues and leaders who have empowered us - that is, trusted us with the freedom and resources to excel - nearly always spur our best performances on.

Google executive Thomas Williams has a great image for grass roots empowerment. Rather than allowing people to be pulled into repetitive 'hamster wheel' tasks, he gives them the freedom to 'build their own treadmills'. That way, he says, 'No one's telling you you're not going fast enough — everyone is telling themselves that.' This kind of respectful empowerment leads to more creativity and risk-taking, boosting the chance that people will enjoy their jobs and that the whole organisation will benefit.

Low-trust organisations have trouble giving their teams the latitude to do much. Wary of everyone, they often don't trust even their most trustworthy people. Instead, they rely on thick compliance manuals for even the most trivial matters, and reward tattlers as a way to prevent rule-breaking. This suspicious atmosphere kills initiative and creativity, and worst of all, it stifles any potential for trust. It's true that neither trust nor power should be bestowed with foresight. As with trust in any area of life, it should be granted to people with the character and competence to make responsible use of it. But at the very least, everyone should have the opportunity to earn it.

Here are a few things to consider if you're aiming to build a culture where people are empowered to do great work:

Bet on people. Allow people a chance to prove they can take on more responsibility. A leader who trusts others to grow, knowing they may stumble, exhibits a level of trust that generally inspires the best in people and can ignite sparks of trust in an otherwise mistrustful environment. Identifying and empowering the most competent, highest-integrity team members is a great way to start.

Take action. That means a preference for trying out ideas, rather than sitting around planning and analysing. In short, when people are actually doing things, iterating and refining as they go, they tend to get the best results. Empowering teams to act means missteps are less expensive and people learn faster.

Don't forget the past. OK - now forget the past. Many organisations do things because 'that's the way it's always been done.' An organisation's 'best practices' are often just organisational scar tissue, the codification of long-forgotten mistakes that are no longer relevant in the current world. High-trust organisations don't rely blindly on old rules. Instead, they trust their teams to figure out the new ones. Remember the phrase – do what you have always done, and you'll get what you have always got.

Expect mistakes. Granting trust doesn't guarantee perfect results. In fact the more latitude you give people, the more you may find they miss the mark as they grow into their responsibilities. Part of trusting team members with power means understanding that even the best efforts can, and do, falter. When it happens, the team should examine the reasons for the misstep, distil some lessons and move forward with renewed vigour.

Avoid the paraphernalia of paranoia. If trust-based organisations focus on empowering people to do their best, mistrustful ones fixate on preventing people from doing their worst. Trust-poor enterprises often assuage their fear of disaster with policy manuals, compliance committees, overactive legal departments, even rewards for turning others in. These practices give rise to an anxious, worst-case mind-set that can squash confidence and creativity, which is commonly inherent in the public sector.

For some leaders, the idea of sharing power feels risky. They may never have learned that giving up power is a great way to create more. That's unfortunate because, in many organisations, those with the best information do not work at headquarters but on the front lines. Organisations that don't trust anyone outside the inner circle are destined to disappoint and stumble, while their high-trust counterparts marshal talent and experience from deep within the ranks.

31

Time to look in the mirror

When you have looked through all the points raised in this book, the final part of the journey is to begin to look at yourself as a leader, business owner or manager and ask yourself what you are doing right and what you are doing wrong. Some of the exercises will have helped engage with your current situation and shown how the development areas are clear for further investigation. Let's never forget that no one gets all of this right in one go, no one wakes up the perfect mentor for their teams - it comes through making mistakes, but also by ultimately ensuring that you notice them, thereby encouraging change for the better.

It certainly helps when working with people to understand your levels of compassion, something rarely identified with buy-in from senior people. I found the book

People by Jo-Ellen Demetrious a great place to understand more about yourself as a manager. There is a discussion of the compassion scale - a simple rule of thumb which can help identify where you are at as a person in the workplace. Remember that different environments may highlight different levels of compassion. For sure when you are with family and friends you may seem the centre of compassionate feelings, but the work environment will bring very diverse feelings which should be looked at on their own merits.

An individual's level of compassion is a good indicator of how people will behave in certain situations. Someone could seem a clear cold, unemotional person, or at the other end of the scale he could be seen as warm and open. The closer the person is to the warmer end of the scale the more they will tend to be generous, fair, sincere, understanding etc, all the traits we look for in a manager when we want to be motivated. They will be inclined to give the benefit of the doubt, being more inquisitive to situations that occur, key motivators we have discussed throughout the chapters on enabling a good flow of communication between levels of the workforce. However this type of person may have more difficulty coming to decisions than those who are less compassionate. This could be seen as common sense, as a little more emotion will go into the final decisions, because at the end of the day they want it right first time.

Those who fall to the other end of the scale fit the 'state not slate' model - critical, intolerant, unforgiving, punitive etc. You may find you adhere to some of these ways and see them as qualities, but nine times out of ten they will create a barrier between staff and management which finds little in the way of success long term. Less compassionate people will be more analytical, most likely scanning facts and making quick 'knee jerk' decisions based on the minimal absorption of information. By the same token you will find less compassionate people tend to be more judgemental, impetuous and inclined to act before all the information is in. It is said that their motto will be along the lines of 'What's in it for me?'

If you begin to highlight yourself, or any of those around you, as either compassionate or unusually cold, you already know more about where you are or where they are than you will from information such as age, education and employment. It can be a key driver for yourself to understand the areas to change and those around who may not change, but at least you can help manage the expectation of your interaction with those people.

So things to look out for on a scale of compassion are as follows:

Compassionate	Non-compassionate
Fair	Critical
Sincere	Intolerant
Affectionate	Unforgiving
Gentle	Harsh
Family orientated	Punitive
Forgiving	Self-centred
Understanding	Judgemental
Benefit of the Doubt	Impetuous
Inquisitive	Indifferent
Patient	Impatient

There are more phrases which can produce a more exhaustive list of examples, but for the purposes of this book just take some time now or later on to examine yourself and those around you. Are you compassionate or not? This could be a key to unlocking your own interpretation of how others see you in the workplace and the relationship you may have because of this approach. The start of redesigning workplace relationships can be understanding your own approach to people, building a platform for re-engagement on a daily basis. It won't happen overnight, but subtle changes in delivery will bring about huge changes in attitudes to help the growth of any business.

SUMMARY

So we reach the end of the book, but not the end of the process. I hope you take some of the points that have been raised and use them in the preparation for your next project or to begin to apply change to the organisation you are with. The link from people to success is everywhere to be seen and creating vibrant process-orientated businesses helps ultimate success, which is indeed business growth.

Remember, 'You don't build a business - You build people, and the people build your business'.

Much of the book refers to great business leaders and simple informative tasks that breed employee lead businesses. In a recent Q&A with Richard Branson he was asked a similar question, which I hope has been summed up throughout this book. It goes as follows:

What advice would you give to a start-up trying to create a healthy and positive culture for their employees?

There's no magic formula. The key is just to treat your staff as you would like to be treated. People want to work on projects that mean something to them, and be surrounded by colleagues who treat them with the respect they deserve. If all companies took this approach, then employee wellbeing ratings would be much higher. (Richard Branson, 2013)

What do you view as the biggest issue that needs addressing in the workplace?

Many companies seem to fail to embrace their staff as individuals. Have you ever received bad news while at work? Have you had a family commitment that has clashed with your job? Whether it's coming in later each morning so that you can drop the children off at school, or taking time out to visit a sick relative, or even a sabbatical to concentrate on other things or recharge – employers should embrace the different needs of each member of staff, rather than try to impose a one-size-fits-all solution to problems. (Richard Branson, 2013)

Two simple yet concise responses to the overall picture of employee engagement, working together to make a business grow and flourish in the way it should. The people we employ are intrinsic to where we want to be as a business, so cherish them, work with them and the end goal will be greater than you could have ever imagined.

Additional Reading

Along the way I have found many books useful, and hopefully you will too. These books have helped in many ways in developing my own businesses and my own personal feelings towards those I work with, and they have added valuable supporting detail to points raised in this book. Some elements have been directly cited, or I have shown models I have utilised to offer a greater internal support to my people.

Books

Eat that frog - Brian Tracey

Four-Hour Work Week - Timothy Ferris

Four-Hour Body - Timothy Ferris

Think and Grow Rich - Napoleon Hill

Rich Dad, Poor Dad - Robert Kiosacki

The One-Minute Manager - Ken Blanchard & Spencer Johnson

7 Habits of Highly Effective People - Stephen R Covey

The Chimp Paradox - Dr Steve Peters

The Ecstasy of Surrender - Judith Orloff MD

Reading People - Jo-Ellen Demetrious

Good to Great - Jim Collins

25596174R00114

Printed in Poland
by Amazon Fulfillment
Poland Sp. z o.o., Wrocław